HEAVEN

HEAVEN

Charles Ferguson Ball

While this book is designed for the reader's personal enjoyment and profit, it is also intended for group study. A Leader's Guide with Victor Multiuse Transparency Masters is available from your local bookstore or from the publisher.

VICTOR BOOKS
a division of SP Publications, Inc.
WHEATON. ILLINOIS 60187

Offices also in Fullerton, California • Whitby, Ontario, Canada • Amersham-on-the-Hill, Bucks, England

Second printing, 1981

Cover photo by Gary Irving

Scripture quotations are taken from the King James Version of the Bible, unless otherwise noted. Other versions used are the *New International Version* (NIV) © 1978 by the New York International Bible Society; *The New Berkeley Version in Modern English* (BERK) © 1945, 1959, 1969 by the Zondervan Publishing House; *The Living Bible* (LB), Tyndale House Publishers, Wheaton, Illinois; *The New Testament in Modern English* (PH), © J.B. Phillips 1958, The Macmillan Company. Used by permission.

Recommended Dewey Decimal Classification: 237
    Suggested Subject Headings: HEAVEN—RESURRECTION

Library of Congress Catalog Card Number: 80-51560
ISBN: 0-89693-004-1

VICTOR BOOKS
A division of SP Publications, Inc.
P.O. Box 1825 • Wheaton, Illinois 60187

To my wife, Catherine,
who for fifty years has walked
hand in hand with me
in the Christian ministry,
and whose unfailing loyalty has
strengthened the cause of Christ.

Contents

Preface

What can we know about heaven? All that the Bible reveals. For all that is known about heaven is in the Bible. Whatever is written about the hereafter is a guess and a speculation unless it is based on God's Word.

The question of a future life is not a scientific inquiry or a mathematical proposition to be proven. It is not a sociological, philosophical, or political question. Rather, it is a religious question. A future life will be spent in a spiritual realm. The person who rejects the Bible's revelation can know nothing for sure about the future.

The late Dr. W.H. Griffith Thomas wisely said, "The consideration of heaven is no mere spiritual luxury, no mere intellectual dissipation, no imaginative revelry, but is really and definitely practical and suitable for the robust thinker and worker as well as for the contemplative mystic, and has a real bearing on our daily life" (*Sunday School Times*).

With firm faith in the Scriptures of the Old and New Testaments, and with hearts aglow in Christ's salvation, we press toward the mark of the calling on high by God in Christ Jesus to heaven, our eternal home.

1

Is There Life After Death?

Today there is great fascination about life after death. Questions about man's final destiny are not always prompted by curiosity. They are more frequently a response to the fact that God has planted eternity within the human heart. Man is restless until the matter is settled and his life hereafter is assured.

In the seventh century, before Christianity came to the land of Britain, Woden and Thunder were the most popular pagan gods. The first Christian to take the Gospel message to the court of Edwin, king of Northumbria, was Paulinas, a follower of Augustine.

As Paulinas entered the court, he saw before him the assembled wise men of the land, whom Edwin had brought together to hear about the new religion.

One of the bearded earls rose and said to Edwin, "So seems the life of man, O King, as a sparrow's flight through the hall where a man is sitting at meat in wintertide, with

11

its warmth, its lights, its laughter; and tarrying but a moment, flies out again with the night and vanishes into the darkness from which it came. So tarries for a moment the life of man in our sight.

"Does the new religion tell us anything of what comes after death? If it does, let us follow it."

The question of the old earl has shaped itself in the mind of man from the beginning. It was the question of Job. "If a man die, shall he live again?" (14:14) It is the question of our hearts today.

Since we live in a vast cosmos, we are bound to ask yet another question: "Is there any purpose in the existence of this universe itself?" If there is no answer to these questions, then life has no meaning and we live in a madhouse.

One hundred years ago, the hope of life after death held a large place in literature and preaching. Wordsworth wrote his "Ode to the Intimations of Immortality," Tennyson, his "In Memoriam," and Browning, his "Daring Ventures into the Unseen." A future life was commonly discussed in learned circles.

Then the popular scientific influence of recent generations changed the emphasis from the next world to this present one, pushing the subject of the hereafter into the background. The note of immortality almost vanished from literature as well as from the pulpit. Only a few years ago, scarcely a clergyman could be found who would preach about heaven or hell. It was thought to be morbid and in poor taste.

Besides, there was so much guessing and speculating on this subject that it was not intellectually acceptable to get involved in things of another world when man had so much yet to learn about this one. Preachers who were forever occupied with the next life were not making full proof of their present ministry. So the note of immortality almost vanished.

But this is rapidly changing. In recent years there has been a revival of interest in, and a plethora of books and magazine articles about, life after death. The subject has moved from the cloister to the curb.

Thanatology, or the science of death, dying, and the hereafter, is now a fad on the market. Discerning Christians do well to look with suspicion on many of the assertions involving the mystical experiences of those who claim to be brought back from death's frontier. Too many of these border on the occult and the satanic, and the Scriptures give specific warnings and even prohibitions against all such. Here is an area that God has not chosen to reveal to us. When we are enticed to go beyond what He has revealed, we are out of our depth and in grave danger. Nothing has ever been established by thanatology that is not already revealed in God's Word.

It should be noted, however, that the current revival in the investigation of the hereafter is not, as might be supposed, the occupation of questionable cults and wild-eyed sensationalists, but of reputable authors and physicians well-known in scholastic circles. Two examples are Arnold Toynbee's *Life After Death* (McGraw, 1976) and Archie Matson's *Afterlife: Reports from the Threshhold of Death*, (Harper and Row, 1977).

More recently, from the medical profession and written from an objective and scientific point of view, have come books which have captured popular attention. They claim to be the result of personal interviews with patients who assert that they were pronounced clinically dead and at the same time were conscious of mysterious experiences which were anything but frightening, and in many instances quite pleasant.

Three such books are *On Death and Dying* by Elisabeth Kubler-Ross, M.D. (Macmillan, 1969), *Life After Life* by Raymond A. Moody, Jr. (Stackpole, 1976), and *Beyond Death's Door* by Maurice Rawlings, M.D. (Nelson, 1978).

Many of the people interviewed claimed to have experienced a feeling of weightlessness, a floating sensation, a passing through a dark tunnel with bright light at the end, and a sense of peace and wholeness.

Interestingly, the authors do not actually claim that these people interviewed were in fact dead, but only that their vital life signs were not detectable. They were presumed dead during their "out-of-the-body experiences."

In a pamphlet on modern thanatology, Mark Albrecht and Brooks Alexander state, "The metaphysics of popular thanatology are in harmony with the discipline's psychedelic roots, which are openly occult and Eastern mystical." They contend that "the message, in essence, is that there is indeed life after death, that it has been scientifically documented, and that joy, reunion, rewards, and fulfillment await everyone on the other side, regardless of one's beliefs, spiritual state, or moral practices here on earth."

Albrecht and Alexander feel the most recent writings of Kubler-Ross and Moody lean heavily on the teachings of Robert Monroe, author of the book *Journeys Out of the Body* (Doubleday, 1977). This book puts such a strain on our limits of credibility that it can hardly be taken seriously.

Today courses are offered in colleges and in churches on death and dying. Agencies exist for counseling in this field, and some preachers are making extravagant claims about people who were allegedly clinically dead but later lived to tell the tale. The motion picture industry has come out with a film titled *Beyond and Back.* Evidently, there is either a great deal of interest being generated in this materialistic culture of ours, or our generation is on the rebound from a humanism that does not satisfy.

We contend that the only answer that does satisfy is found in the Bible and ultimately in the miracle of Christ's resurrection from the grave. From the Christian point of view, one of the most personal and discerning treatments of the whole matter of death and dying was written by Joseph Bayly, titled, *The View from a Hearse* (Cook, 1969).

Since the subject is vast, there is danger of pursuing it in such miscellaneous commentary as to run on and on, far beyond the patience of our readers. We will, therefore, confine ourselves to those things revealed in Holy Scripture. Without a revelation from God, no one knows anything about the life to come. All else is a guess and, no matter how comforting, a speculation.

Life after death is very much a spiritual matter. To a dying thief, Christ Jesus said, "Today shalt thou be with Me in paradise" (Luke 23:43). How very certain He was! He did not say, "I hope we shall meet again, " or "We may well suppose there is a hereafter." He said, "Today you will be with Me in paradise." What a fraudulent thing to say, if He was not sure!

While it is true that much—very much—is "seen only through a glass darkly," it is gloriously true that much has been revealed; and it is our privilege and our duty to find out all we can about it and then wait until the clouds are rolled away and faith has become sight.

2

What Are the Intimations of Immortality?

Few people really believe that death is the end of their existence. No grave has been packed so tightly but that out of it does not come the question: "Is there a life hereafter?"

Belief in a life after death seems to be inherent in man's very nature. In the Book of Ecclesiastes, we read that God "has set eternity in the hearts of men" (3:11,NIV). That fact becomes evident when we study the religions and philosophies of all races. Belief may occur in varying degrees of vagueness or of clarity, but it is there.

In life the one ultimate mystery that looms larger than all others is the question of the hereafter. It is the one question that will not down. If we try to persuade ourselves that it really does not matter, our voices have a hollow ring. If we try to argue that this life is all, we are inundated with so many unanswered questions, so many dead-end conclusions, and so much anguish that our very existence here becomes a blunder, "a tale told by an idiot, full of sound and fury, signifying nothing," as Shakespeare's Macbeth said, after he learned of the queen's death. If we have only this life, spare us from it.

What Does Life Mean?

In childhood years we were not interested in the hereafter any more than a five-year-old is interested in the stock market. There were other things to do, such as acquiring toys and teddy bears. Later came the tricycle and the football helmet and schooling. Then falling in love, the birth of our children, the raising of a family, and finally the burdens of old age. And so our tale is told!

In the questioning years of high school and college, when we knew vastly more about all things than our elders, we could, at the drop of the hat, debate the question, "Is there life after death?" It was an enticing mental gymnastic to bring forth all the strong reasons for the immortality of the soul, but it was only an exercise and exceedingly academic.

But with maturity in years comes the realization that life here is brief at best. "To every mother's son of us death cometh soon or late." We discover that values change and mysteries multiply. As we near the boundary between this life and the next, we notice that more of our friends and loved ones are missing, and our interest in the hereafter increases. It is a vested interest now, for payday draws near.

What is life all about? Those radiant days of growing up, those years of learning facts and acquiring wisdom, working hard to reach security, then marriage and children and the responsibilities of home, the stormy billows of life's middle passage, the plans, the hopes, the dreams, and then the sunset and night! What is it all about? Has it any meaning or purpose?

Mark Twain was a great humorist and a national hero, but he himself had a dim view of life. In his autobiography he expressed this thought:

The burden of pain, care, misery grows heavier year by year. At length ambition is dead, pride is dead, vanity is dead, longing for release is in their place. It comes at last—the only unpoisoned gift earth ever had for them—and they vanish from a world where they were of no consequence; where they achieved nothing; where they were a mistake and a failure and a foolishness.

What Does Death Mean?

No life is so little or so meaningless, and no death so appalling but that its very atmosphere is vibrant with hope. Long before the Bible confirmed this hope, man felt sure that there was a new day dawning for the soul that closed its eyes on the scenes of earth. What else was the meaning of burying food and furniture in the tombs of the pharaohs?

Cicero once said, "There is in the mind of man a certain presentiment of immortality, and this takes the deepest root and is most discoverable in the greatest geniuses and the most exalted souls."

In one degree or another, some sort of belief in the future life is a universal phenomenon. Even the savage possesses the consciousness that there is something within him that thinks and wills and loves and hates and feels, and that at death this thinking, feeling, willing something persists in a "happy hunting ground" somewhere. This can hardly be called a proof of survival, but it demonstrates that the belief exists in us all.

From the royal tombs of the pharaohs in the pyramids, it is clear that the Egyptians believed in a future life. To provide for their kings in the next world, they stored food and grains, utensils, furniture, weapons, wigs, and mirrors. But theirs was a superstitious hope, with no proof anywhere!

In the cradle of civilization, the Euphrates Valley, the Babylonians and the Assyrians read the signs in the heavens and said there was a large dark cavern below the earth where all the dead were gathered for a miserable existence of inactivity. Occasionally, a favored individual was permitted to escape to a pleasant island. Usually, rulers were singled out for this honor, but few there were to receive it. It was a dark hope, without proof.

The Greek philosophers argued for the indestructibility of the soul. Socrates, with clear logic, contended for it. Plato postulated that because we came from some previous existence, it was necessary to believe in a future existence. His logic was impressive, but he had no proof.

Among the Aztecs and Toltecs of Mexico and Central America, as well as among the Incas of Peru, a vague but persistent belief in the hereafter is evident from their records. But it was only a hope and far from proof.

Immanuel Kant found it essential to accept the idea of immortality as a necessary presupposition of the mortal life. William James said, "We are functions of the cosmos, and when the bodily functions cease in death, it is reasonable that some other link may come in and do the work hitherto done by the body." How vague!

An English scientist, Professor Tyndall, who rejected revelation, nevertheless said "In my highest moods, the hope of immortality is strong within me."

Deep in the heart of mankind is an instinct that death

does not end it all. Such instinct cannot be ignored. It tells that man is spiritual in essence and has been endowed with a capacity for knowing God.

It must be so! Plato, thou reasonest well,
Else whence this pleasing hope, this fond desire,
This longing after immortality?
Or whence this secret dread and inward horror
Of falling into naught? Why shrinks the soul
Back on herself and startles at destruction?
'Tis the Divinity that stirs within us;
'Tis heaven itself that points out a hereafter,
And intimates eternity to man. Joseph Addison, *Cato*

Of course, there have always been intellectuals who sought to deny a hereafter. The Sadducees of Israel constituted a sizable group who rejected any belief in life after death. They were the materialists of Christ's day, and their leaven has permeated the ages to this very hour. Jesus warned, "Beware of the leaven . . . of the Sadducees" (Matt. 16:6).

There are people who boast that they have no desire for life after death. This life has been such a struggle that cessation would be a consummation profoundly to be desired. But this makes of death an escape hatch after a life that offers no reason for human existence in the first place.

There are flippant souls who declare that they are not interested in pearly gates or golden streets, or in what Reinhold Niebuhr sarcastically called "the furniture of heaven and the temperature of hell." Mark Twain in his characteristic way shrugged it all off by quipping, "You take heaven. I'd rather go to Bermuda."

However, with all man's show of rationalism, belief in life after death is still instinctive in human nature. Man inevitably faces the mystery of death seeking some solution. If no clear answer comes, then a strange mood possesses him. He boldly says he is interested in only one world at a time, and that it is all he can do to give this life his full attention.

But the person who takes only one world into consideration makes a shipwreck of both worlds. To exist is magnificent. It is so sublime that it becomes unthinkable to put the boundary on life of three score years and ten, and end it there. The true meaning of life lies out beyond that, and the ultimate value of today's experiences, be they happy or harrowing, is in the Christian view of life eternal.

The Answer

In the Christian context, life has dimensions and meanings which our limited three-dimensional minds can scarcely grasp. "Eye hath not seen, nor ear heard, neither have entered into the heart of man, the things which God hath prepared for them that love Him" (1 Cor. 2:9). Our Lord's promise of life eternal is not only the central hope of life— it is the only answer that makes sense and satisfies the questing heart. Without it, all the best we know in life of truth and beauty and harmony and wisdom is at last utterly lost. Without it, this amazing cosmic world becomes irrational and life itself futile. Christ alone puts sense and meaning into life. If death ends all, surely life is a clumsy jest, and all human values vanish.

In the ancient Book of Job, there is a very trenchant question that Job voiced for us all: "If a man die, shall he live again?" (14:14) It is a question that will not down. Shrug it off as you will, it will meet you again around some dark unguarded corner. It is the cry of humanity.

If we could only be sure that death is not the end, but rather a passing into another stage of conscious existence, no more mysterious than birth when man came out of the warm womb into a new and strange existence.

If we could only be sure of this, then life with all its questions could make sense, and even our sufferings and sorrows would be bearable.

But *can* we be sure that death is not the end? Reason and logic say, "Surely there must be a future life, else there is no purpose for this one."

Science says, "There is no proof from direct observation of experimentation."

Humanity's cry is: "There must be a land beyond the sunset and the night." There is a groaning of the spirit. There is a capacity for God and for eternity.

Job found sufficient answer to satisfy his longings for immortality. In the midst of his sufferings, he exclaimed, "I know that my Redeemer liveth, and that He shall stand at the latter day upon the earth; and though after my skin worms destroy this body, yet in my flesh shall I see God; whom I shall see for myself, and mine eyes shall behold, and not another" (Job 19:25-27).

However, there was no finally definitive answer to Job's question until Jesus Christ our Saviour abolished death and brought life and immortality to light through the Gospel. Into the darkness that lingered around the concept of immortality, Christ brought light like the blazing of the sun. He wrestled with death, went down into its depths, and by rising from the grave conquered it.

The ultimate answer to the question of Job is the risen Christ, who declares, "I am the Resurrection, and the Life" (John 11:25). The only proof of life after death is in the fact that our Saviour rose from the grave and said to His own, "Because I live, ye shall live also" (John 14:19).

Since then, and only since then, have we been able to say, "O Death, where is thy sting? O Grave, where is thy victory?" (1 Cor. 15:55) With these words, the great Apostle Paul taunted death and the grave, saying to death, "You thought you had me, didn't you? But you don't!"

"Thanks be to God, who giveth us the victory through our Lord Jesus Christ" (15:57).

To man's reason the world to come is mysterious beyond human ability to penetrate, but to the Christian it is not. In the resurrection of Christ, God has lifted the veil. Eternal life is now a fact revealed and demonstrated.

What Is Heaven? Is It Real?

Science is not the only source of knowledge. There is another kind of knowledge by which our lives are ordered. And this knowledge cannot be demonstrated in a test tube.

• We know that it is better to be generous and unselfish than to be greedy and grasping, but we cannot prove it.

• We know that Michelangelo is a better artist than Aunt Lizzie, but we cannot demonstrate it.

• We are sure that Shakespeare is a better poet than Cousin Joe, and Bach a better musician than Brother Barney, but we cannot verify it.

There is an intuitive understanding, a natural insight, and a perception of the rightness of things that is more important to our lives than what is demonstrated by science. This knowledge is extrasensory, related perhaps to the subconscious, and to which we answer in faith.

Whatever is beyond our ability to touch, taste, hear, see, or smell is a matter of faith. And faith is not less reasonable than physics or chemistry. In fact, we can never have exact scientific knowledge of anything that relates to the future. We are not certain that the sun will rise tomorrow morning. Of course it always has, and we expect it will again. But we have no proof. We accept it in faith, and we believe such faith is solid. The odds against the sun failing to rise are enormous, but still we have no proof, for some cosmic collision could change the daily pattern.

We do not hesitate, therefore, in saying that faith is a necessity for our understanding of heaven. When we are sure of God and accept His Word, we have a source of knowledge just as valid as the tables of arithmetic. And the mysteries of the future life are unlocked more and more as our faith increases.

Heaven Is a Place

Some people talk about heaven as they would about an imaginary place. They do it with tongue in cheek and a knowing smile, as if to say heaven is a human invention, a never-never land, a realm of dreams, and not to be taken seriously. Others say heaven is a benevolent state of mind, a vague vacuum, or a reward for being good. Some say heaven or hell is what you make of this life—a projection of the best in yourself. Such people believe in the immortality of beauty and truth and influence and memory. But heaven as a place? Never!

If God had intended that this vagueness be the normal response to the question, He would not have allowed so much to be said on the subject in Holy Scripture.

Heaven *is* a place—God's dwelling place. In 1 Kings 8:30, we read, "Hearken Thou to the supplication of Thy servant, and of Thy people Israel, when they shall pray toward this place [the temple]; and hear Thou in heaven Thy dwelling place; and when Thou hearest, forgive." Did not Jesus teach us to say, "Our Father who art in heaven"? Heaven is a place, just as much a place as is New York or Chicago. It is the place where Christ went at His ascension and from which He will come again.

At death the Christian, who by faith becomes one with Christ, will go to be with Him. The purpose of our Lord's return is that He may receive us to Himself so that where He is, we might be also.

It is quite useless to ask for a map of heaven or to try to chart it by latitude and longitude, as we mark out places on the earth. It cannot be located in terms of geography. For space is measured by distance, and distance is calculated from the material conditions of bodies, and these have nothing in common with spiritual beings. Spirit beings have no "whereness." In heaven we will not depend on the experiences or energies known in this life.

But while we can little imagine what the next world will be like for the Christian, yet we can know its reality and the intelligible principles by which it is governed. In heaven we will be like Christ, for we shall be with Him and see Him as He is. (See 1 John 3:2.) Since this implies a condition of which we have no experience on earth, the only way we can know about it is if it is expressed in language that we understand. For example, Jesus said to His disciples, "In My Father's house are many mansions" (John 14:2). The new translations change it to "rooms" or "dwelling places," and even "igloos" in the Eskimo Bible, because Eskimos who had never traveled would have had no conception of a mansion.

To the aged Apostle John, God revealed many of the

glories of our eternal home. In the Book of Revelation, John undertook to tell us something of what he saw in his vision. He was an exile on the Isle of Patmos, for the Gospel's sake, when he heard a voice saying, "'I am Alpha and Omega, the first and the last;' and, 'What thou seest, write in a book, and send it unto the seven churches which are in Asia'" (Rev. 1:11).

John's vision continued: "After this I looked, and, behold, a door was opened in heaven. And the first voice which I heard was as it were of a trumpet talking with me; which said, 'Come up hither, and I will show thee things which must be hereafter'" (4:1).

In an attempt to describe the indescribable, John set down the vision and the experience he had, in the only vehicle possible—human language. He described glories which we have no ability to comprehend. Little wonder then that John used an extravaganza of speech that staggers human imagination. Heaven is too splendid for our human hearts and too vast for our finite minds. So we see only gleams of glory: The street of the city was of pure gold, like transparent glass. . . . The wall was made of jasper. . . . the twelve gates were pearls, each gate made of a single pearl. (See Revelation 21:18-21.) This is far beyond us, but through it all emerges the realization that what John saw is vastly more wonderful than human words can portray.

John's description contains some of the most powerful imagery in the Bible. It is imagery that has deeply affected Christian art and literature, music and piety, in every age. Saints of all the centuries have based their ideas of heaven on this vision, and have found comfort for old age and in times of bereavement. On the plans and specifications from the Book of Revelation, John Bunyan modeled his Celestial

City. The Holy City has inspired much of our poetry and many of our hymns:

> Ten thousand times ten thousand
> In sparkling raiment bright,
> The armies of the ransomed saints
> Throng up the steeps of light.
> 'Tis finished, all is finished,
> Their fight with death and sin;
> Fling open wide the golden gates
> And let the victors in.

No one has an accurate picture of heaven. Even John did not claim that the Book of Revelation contained a blueprint. What he gave us is a description of a heavenly place in earthly terms. But the gold and the pearls, the crowns and the songs, the trees and fruit, and the river and the sea of glass are not the chief attractions of the city. They are only the symbols of its glory. Its central glory is God. Its chief attraction is Christ. Its supreme beauty is spiritual, not material.

Paul himself claimed the amazing experience of being caught up into heaven. He spoke of it as "the third heaven" or "paradise" (2 Cor. 12:1-4). Was this a physical experience or was he in heaven only in a spiritual sense? Paul said he did not know himself: "Whether in the body, I cannot tell; or whether out of the body, I cannot tell; God knoweth." We can be sure it was a time of incredible ecstasy and uncommon rapture. "The third heaven" is a Hebrew expression for the place where the saints and angels are. "Caught up into paradise" is an equivalent expression, and what we mean when we speak of heaven.

In Hebrew thinking, the first heaven was the atmosphere; the second was the stellar spaces; and the third lay beyond the stars, where Christ is seated on the right hand of God the Father, and where the perfected saints live. (See Heb. 12:22-24.) Paul called these experiences "surpassingly great revelations" and concluded that such experiences could make one proud. "To keep me from becoming conceited . . . there was given me a thorn in my flesh" (2 Cor. 12:7, NIV).

Paul said that he heard "inexpressible things, things that man is not permitted to tell" (12:4, NIV), "words too sacred to tell, which no human being is allowed to repeat" (BERK); "words that cannot, and indeed must not, be put into human speech" (PH); "things so astounding that they are beyond a man's power to describe or put in words (and anyway I am not allowed to tell them to others)" (LB).

So Paul never did try. In all his epistles, he was silent about these words he heard in heaven. Fourteen years passed, and Paul never told about them. But because of this experience, he was positive that heaven is a glory land that exceeds anything we could ever know on earth. Comparing life here with the glories of the hereafter, he said that to depart this life and be with Christ was much better. (See Phil. 1:23.)

It is interesting that while today so many are clambering to tell of their visions and experiences of life after death with its light at the end of the dark tunnel, Paul, the great apostle, should have remained silent. For this high experience, he knew that no human words would be adequate.

What Is Heaven Like?

Heaven is not merely a thought form. It is not simply a projection of the best in ourselves. It is not a vision of a longed-for utopia. It is not a pleasing hope or an invention of man. Our own thoughts do not make heaven. Rather, it is a prepared place for a prepared people. Jesus said, "Rejoice, and be exceeding glad; for great is your reward in heaven" (Matt. 5:12).

Paul tells us that our citizenship "is in heaven; whence also we look for the Saviour, the Lord Jesus Christ; who shall change our vile body, that it may be fashioned like unto His glorious body" (Phil. 3:20-21). A person who never thinks of the next life and is not interested in heaven must be cursed with stupidity or plagued with frivolity.

But many questions come to mind:
- Where is heaven located?
- What are its occupations?
- Who will be there?
- What is the manner of its life?
- Shall we know each other there?

These are only a few of the queries that press for an answer. They are not merely academic. Nor are they speculative. They voice the deepest longings of the soul and testify to the basic hunger of our human hearts. And this very hunger is one of the strong proofs that life's pilgrimage does not end at the river of death. The truth is that we all desire a better country than what we know here, a heavenly country (Heb. 11:16.)

Perhaps our greatest mistake as we think of heaven is to make it so supremely material. In the teaching of Christ, it is supremely spiritual. We tend to forget that when we someday put on immortality, these spirits of ours will find very little happiness in golden pavements and pearly gates. We all know people who have had wealth in abundance and yet have never been happy. Material things cannot guarantee eternal joys, for we do not live by gold and jasper, or even by bread alone, but by every word that proceeds out of the mouth of God.

Heaven is not only a place where we will go, but something we will be! Although we think of it as *somewhere*, first of all it is *Somebody*. We so easily forget that Christ is heaven, and heaven is Christ. Heaven is union with God. A heaven somewhere outside of ourselves has no meaning unless we have a heaven within.

Yes, that grand vision in the Revelation is an *anthropomorphism*, or an interpretation of what is not human in terms of human or earthly characteristics. The vision has its meanings, but its first true message is not materialistic. Hidden in every wall and gate and stone and street is the deeper message for which the material is only the symbol.

For the city itself is the symbol of a community and indicates togetherness and fellowship. No life is perfect without fellowship. Without fellowship there is only existence, not fullness of life. Thank God we will be with Him and with one another in the glory, as a heavenly community, in a city whose Builder and Maker is God. And within that fellowship, we will know and recognize one another in holy companionship and communion.

• The *walls* of the city signify security and separation. All ancient cities were walled to keep out intruders and to protect against invasion. Behind the walls the inhabitants dwelt safely, free from fear of attack, for John says, "Without are dogs, and sorcerers, and whoremongers, and murderers, and idolaters, and whosoever loveth and maketh a lie" (Rev. 22:15). And there shall not enter into it "anything that defileth, neither whatsoever worketh abomination, or maketh a lie; but they which are written in the Lamb's

Book of Life" (21:27).

• The open *gates* suggest the sympathy and generosity of the soul made perfect. "And the gates of it shall not be shut at all by day; for there shall be no night there" (21:25). Here is true communion between the redeemed ones.

• The crystal-clear, pure *river* of water of life symbolizes the pure joy of the holy life. It is a quality of living as yet unfamiliar to earthlings, who have by inheritance a sin nature and whose life here has been characterized by a warfare going on between the old nature and the new. Holiness is an attribute of Almighty God. It is not a natural attribute of man. But when God's plan for us is complete, we shall be like Him. Then we shall be truly sanctified.

• The white *robes* are badges of stainless purity. The linen of the priests' garments is white. Everywhere in the Bible, white is the emblem of purity. In Revelation 19:8 we read of the bride at the marriage of the Lamb, that "to her was granted that she should be arrayed in fine linen, clean and white; for the fine linen is the righteousness of the saints."

Life in heaven will be characterized by purity. What a contrast to life here, which is characterized by imperfection, sin, and weakness. "All have sinned, and come short of the glory of God" (Rom. 3:23). But in heaven we will be pure. A great many find flaws in our character down here, but one day Christ will present us before the Father "not having spot or wrinkle," but complete in Him (Eph. 5:27).

• The *crowns* and *palms* are emblems of victory. At last we shall triumph by God's grace. The battle is over, the long struggle ended.

• *Gold*, *jasper*, and *pearls* express the riches of heaven, for they are human symbols of wealth. While they are not necessarily divine standards, their use makes it clear that there is no poverty in heaven. In fact, we are encouraged to lay up for ourselves treasures in our eternal home. (See Matt. 6:20.)

• The *songs* and the *music* of harps and feasting mean abounding happiness and joy such as we have never known, and fervent thanksgiving for all the goodness of God. We will sing a new song, the song of Moses and of the Lamb.

In this life, we have heard glorious music which has lifted us to the gates of heaven. Handel, after he had finished *The Messiah*, said, "Methinks I did see all heaven open before me and the great God Himself. . . . I think God has visited me." But the singing we have on earth is nothing compared with the songs of that other world, for all discord will be done away with. Harmony such as we have never known will characterize that life.

This then is the central idea of heaven—fellowship with God in a place that our Saviour is now making ready for us. And when we are changed into His likeness, we will have new standards, new values, new joys, new songs, new powers, a new heart, new life, new loyalties, new understanding, a new world, and a new home.

There is no doubt that heaven is a place. Jesus said, "I go to prepare a place for you . . . that where I am, there you may be also" (John 14:2-3). It is idle to speculate just where that place is, though some have placed it "in the sides of the north," claiming that north is "up" from everywhere on the earth. It could well be that a corner of it might be this old earth of ours, where we toiled and wept and suffered and found our precious Lord. In the great renovation that shall sweep the universe, when there shall be a new heaven and a new earth, the very world in which we live will be purified. The curse of sin will be lifted; the blight on nature gone; Satan, the lord of wrong, dispossessed and banished; and the love of Christ shall reign supreme. Then the Spirit of God shall occupy man's heart, and it will be heaven indeed.

4

What Will You Be Like in Heaven?

Although most people believe in some kind of life after death, they do not all have the Christian assurance of resurrection. Many people misunderstand Christian belief in life after death, regarding it as a vague endorsement of the almost universal hope for the immortality of the soul. Christian hope for the hereafter is much more than that, for it promises the resurrection of the body.

In the shadow of the Temple of Athena in Athens, a small group of Greek philosophers deigned to listen to the words of an unknown Jew who seemed to them "to be a setter-forth of strange gods" (Acts 17:18). They possessed a typical Greek reverence for knowledge and revelled in the prospect of hearing some new thing. That Jew was the Apostle Paul. The place was Mars Hill.

Paul's text was an inscription seen on an altar in an Athens street, "To the Unknown God." His message was that God our Father has called all men to repentance through

Jesus Christ, by whom He will one day judge the world. The evidence for this is that God raised Jesus from the dead.

Paul had the distinction of introducing something new to the Greeks of Athens. It was the doctrine of the resurrection of the body.

These Greek men were well versed in philosophy and indeed were living at the very throne of the world's culture. Until the final point in Paul's sermon, they had at least shown interest, but the curiosity that caused them to hear him patiently was growing thin. Suddenly, it turned to scorn and joking, as most of them went their ways, wagging their heads and affirming that they had wasted their time with such a fool.

Their problem was that they were not ready to receive this new doctrine—the resurrection of the body. Had Paul merely said that the soul would live after death, there would have been no question. But who had ever heard of a body being raised from the dead, except in mythology? It was not only impossible; it was unthinkable.

And so say some intellectuals of our own day. They argue from the book of science; and from that authority, they are correct, for most of the textbooks agree!

The Meaning of the Body

It was characteristic of Greek philosophy to despise the body as the source of sin. The human body was frequently regarded as a prison, from which death would release a person.

Paul wrote many of his epistles to correct the theories of the Gnostics. They based their philosophy on the premise that there were only two realities: spirit and matter. These two were in conflict, they said. Since matter was evil, the body must be evil. Any notion that the body could be immortal would have severely damaged their whole system of philosophy. The doctrine of the Incarnation—that God took upon Himself a human body and revealed Himself in Jesus Christ—was unthinkable. For that reason Jesus, who was obviously human, could not be divine. Paul had argued that "in Him dwelleth all the fullness of the Godhead bodily" (Col. 2:9). With their gnostic view in mind, the men Paul encountered at the Areopagus regarded the resurrection of the body as the worst thing that could happen.

Before Jesus Christ came, belief in the resurrection of the body was less defined than it is now. Jesus' resurrection was the turning point. For His disciples became so convinced of His physical resurrection that they were willing to die as martyrs rather than deny that conviction.

No man will die for what he knows to be a hoax. He might be led to perpetrate such a deception just so long as he is getting something out of it—wealth or fame perhaps. But when the sword is at his throat and the choice is "Recant or die," there is nothing more to be gained. It is the glory of Christianity that thousands gave their lives, esteeming it a distinction to die for what they knew was the truth.

The Resurrection of the Body

What do we mean by the resurrection of the body? We mean that God raises up persons from death in bodily form and fashions them anew, fitting them for a place and a life that flesh and blood cannot inherit. This body of the resurrection is what Paul calls the "house which is from heaven" (2 Cor. 5:2).

The limitation of our present knowledge makes it almost impossible to comprehend the resurrection of a body. We raise questions about flesh that is buried in a grave and reduced to the elements, or burned to ashes, or dissolved in the sea. Can it be possible that these scattered elements will be reassembled with the same molecular structure as at the hour of death? Some have ridiculed this by picturing a body in the grave, dissolving in the action of the rain and the heat of the sun, and in time fertilizing the grass above, where a cow is grazing. But the cow produces milk, which is consumed at the breakfast table and nourishes another generation. The problem will be, in the resurrection, to decide which molecules belong to which person! All of this is ridiculous and reveals a complete misunderstanding of the Bible. It comes from thinking only in terms of the natural and the physical, with no understanding of the spiritual.

Constant change is going on in the cells of our bodies in this life. We are not the same as we were three years ago. Cells of our bodies are being thrown off each day and other new cells are taking their places. We once were told that each seven years our every cell is renewed. Now scientists claim it is every three years, and yet we do not lose identity. We are the same persons with the same individuality as we were twenty or fifty years ago, even though we do not have the same bodies molecularly. A person of fifty has worn out more than sixteen bodies but is still the same person.

If this renewal is so in our earthly span, why is it so difficult to believe that God has something better for us, a body suited for an eternal order?

Perhaps you knew your grandfather in his last years as a very old man, stooped and arthritic. Will his resurrection body be stooped and arthritic?

If your baby was taken from you in infancy, you still sorrow at the thought of that little body you tenderly laid in the grave. In the resurrection, will that child be like the baby you buried? If not, how will you recognize one another? The pagans mocked the Christians, saying, "Shall we go thither with hair on our heads and nails on our fingers?" These questions are coarse gibes that answer nothing.

Paul met these same questions head-on when he wrote, "Someone may ask, 'How are the dead raised? With what kind of body will they come?' How foolish! What you sow does not come to life unless it dies" (1 Cor. 15:35-36, NIV).

Paul was asking them to consider the miracle of the harvest. It truly is a miracle, but custom dulls its wonder. From the seed in the earth, dying and decaying, rises again the same grain in a rich and a glorious harvest.

Paul did not claim that the actual body which is laid in a grave will be the resurrection body. In fact in his resurrection parable he said, "When you sow, you do not plant the body that will be, but just a seed" (v. 37, NIV). In some way, beyond our present understanding, a new body will rise, changed and fitted for a life that transcends this mundane sphere, and made ready for the fellowship with God that was intended by Him, had not sin come in to destroy the picture. Life is indestructible. And by God's supernatural power, life will be transformed and reclothed in a new body, a spiritual body, like the resurrection body of our Lord. For us who belong to the family of faith, the resurrection powers of Christ are the key to our comprehension of life after death.

Resurrection means the giving of a new kind of body

fitted for heaven. And that body will be the organ to express our personality, just as our present mortal body expresses it here. Paul called that new body a *spiritual body,* meaning that it is not flesh and blood as we know it, but is suited to a new and better life in a new land called heaven. "Our citizenship is in heaven. And we eagerly await a Saviour from there, the Lord Jesus Christ, who, by the power that enables Him to bring everything under His control, will transform our lowly bodies so that they will be like His glorious body" (Phil. 3:20-21, NIV).

The greatest statement on the resurrection life in the whole Bible was given by revelation to Paul:

That which thou sowest is not quickened, except it die. And that which thou sowest, thou sowest not that body that shall be, but bare grain, it may chance of wheat, or of some other grain. But God giveth it a body as it hath pleased Him, and to every seed his own body. . . . So also is the resurrection of the dead. It is sown in corruption; it is raised in incorruption. It is sown in dishonor; it is raised in glory. It is sown in weakness; it is raised in power. It is sown a natural body; it is raised a spiritual body" (1 Cor. 15:36-38, 42-44).

Paul's answer is so clear that it is blinding! "Thou fool, that which thou sowest is not quickened, except it die" (v. 36). It is a natural body which is laid in the ground where its outward form rots and decays, and yet the wheat reappears in a new life. The nature of the seed has not changed. It is still wheat, but it has a new body suited to a new life and new surroundings and circumstances. "So also is the resurrection of the dead" (v. 42).

Our resurrection body is a spiritual body. It is imperishable, for there is no element of death in it. The great enemy—

man's last enemy—is vanquished, and life takes on a different character. Death is missing! Glory hallelujah! "The last enemy that shall be destroyed is death" (15:26).

When he saw the Holy City, the Apostle John wrote, "And God shall wipe away all tears from their eyes; and there shall be no more death, neither sorrow nor crying, neither shall there be any more pain, for the former things are passed away" (Rev. 21:4).

But what is a spiritual body like? We have never seen a spiritual body. Paul explained that it will be like Christ's glorious body. It will be conformed to the image of God's Son. "Beloved," wrote John, "now are we the sons of God, and it doth not yet appear what we shall be; but we know that when He shall appear, we shall be like Him, for we shall see Him as He is" (1 John 3:2).

Christ's resurrection body is the pattern for us. Jesus in His resurrection became "the firstfruits of them that slept" (1 Cor. 15:20). He is the prophecy and the model for the full harvest which shall follow in that glorious day. What superb logic and inspiration are found in Paul's magnificent metaphor! No wonder he could shout, "O Death, where is thy sting? O Grave, where is thy victory?" (15:55)

Three Who Were There

In all ages, it has been said that of the myriads of men and women who have entered the dark gates of death, not one has ever returned to tell us where the dead are or of what their life consists. The inference of the statement is: "Isn't it all a guess? Isn't it all wishful thinking?"

With a Bible in our hand, we deny the claim that no one has returned. There are at least three who have told us something of the land beyond the sunset and the night.

• The first, of course, is none other than our Lord Jesus Christ, whose home was heaven, who was in the glory with the Father before the world was. He spoke as familiarly about heaven as you and I speak of our earthly homes. He called it "My Father's house." He said that in His Father's house there were many mansions, dwelling places, rooms. Jesus had a lot to say about heaven, and He said it with authority, for He had experienced its glory before the world was.

• The second Bible character who had been in heaven was the Apostle Paul. How wonderful it would be if we could read the record of what Paul saw and heard in heaven! It would surely answer many of our questions and resolve our speculations.

Even though he didn't record his experience, we learn more from Paul about the nature of the heavenly life than from any other writer in the Bible. He captures our attention by saying, "We know that if our earthly house of this tabernacle were dissolved, we have a building of God, a house not made with hands, eternal in the heavens" (2 Cor. 5:1). In these great figures of speech where Paul likened death to exchanging a tent for a palace, he set forth the great certainty of all believers—the permanent building of God, the house not made with hands.

• The third person who had experienced heaven was John, author of the Book of Revelation. He was given a view of heaven that is beyond imagination. Picture his dilemma. He had seen the glories of that eternal home but had only human language to describe it. His readers would possess only three-dimensional minds to grasp a vision of infinite dimensions. No wonder he exhausted speech and imagination in an extravaganza of words to describe some-

thing wonderful that we have no mental powers to fully grasp or appreciate. "Streets paved with pure gold, clear as crystal!" Surely that is different than any gold we have ever seen.

If you had seen the glories of another world and then had come back to earth where we all gathered around you and asked, "What was it like?" you would understand John's difficulty. You would no doubt summon for your use the most precious things you knew on earth in a vain attempt to say it all. Golden streets; pearly gates; no need of the sun but instead the light of God's glory; jasper and sapphire and emerald and onyx and beryl and amethyst. Who made these so precious in God's sight? Obviously they are precious by human standards, expressing value in a way we understand. Whatever heaven is like, we have no equipment to appreciate it now. But we know it must far exceed our wildest dreams and our most extravagant thoughts.

The Supernatural Body

A new body—a spiritual body—that too is hard to understand. The nearest we can come to a satisfying apprehension of this is what we know of the risen Christ. When He appeared to His disciples, they recognized Him. He was in the form and visage which they had known for some three years. To doubting Thomas, He openly displayed the marks of His wounds, saying, "Reach hither thy finger, and behold My hands; and reach hither thy hand, and thrust it into My side; and be not faithless, but believing" (John 20:27).

At the same time, there was something different about Jesus' body. It was supernatural. There were times when His followers did not recognize it. Mary thought she was

speaking to the gardener. The two disciples on the road to Emmaus failed to recognize Him until they watched Him break the bread. That supernatural body could pass through the walls of a room where the doors and windows were barred for fear of the Jews. It could suddenly appear and then transport itself to distant places, as one who is omnipresent. Yet in that body, the risen Christ partook of food by the shore of Galilee and in the home at Emmaus. Mystery? Yes, beyond human comprehension, and blinding in its splendor!

Our minds cannot conceive the nature of the spiritual body through which our personality will function in heaven. We see all this now in a glass darkly, but will one day exchange our surroundings and our situations for a happiness such as can never be experienced here. David expressed it this way: "In Thy presence is fullness of joy; at Thy right hand there are pleasures forevermore" (Ps. 16:11).

Benjamin Franklin in his epitaph wrote of this present body which, he said, lies in the grave like the cover of an old book with its contents torn out and stripped of its lettering, but which will appear once again, in a new and more eloquent edition, revised and corrected by the Author.

Just as "the body of our humiliation" has been the servant of our spirit in this life, so the new spiritual body, raised in glory and power, will be the agent of the redeemed spirit. Surely, if man in his corruptible body has been able to achieve so much, his new spiritual, incorruptible, glorified body will be able to do much more. For this reason among others, we believe there will be a higher and better recognition of our loved ones and of all God's children in the redeemed family. It is unthinkable that in heaven we

will know less than we do here. "For now we see through a glass, darkly; but then face to face. Now I know in part; but then shall I know even as also I am known" (1 Cor. 13:12).

Salvation is a regeneration of persons. The complete person consists of body, soul, and spirit. Since we do not know what a person is apart from our earthly experience of him as an individual, we believe and expect that God in some way will make it possible for us to know each other after death. Our happiness depends so much on our fellowship with each other that it is difficult to see how heaven could be heaven unless this is so.

To the sorrowing Martha, Jesus said, "Thy brother shall rise again" (John 11:23). The comfort for Mary and Martha was in the fact that Lazarus would still be recognized as their brother. Immortality without memory or recognition would be formidable and fearful. It is only at death that we who are Christians begin to realize what real life is. It is a life of incredible joy and blessedness, of communion with God and His redeemed ones, and beyond our capacity to imagine.

5

What Is a Spiritual Body? Is It Substantial?

Yesterday in our world, well over 100,000 people died, some in warfare, some by accident, but most by natural causes. Death is life's major crisis, for it ends relationships. Try as we will to speak poetically of it as gentle, sweet, or soothing, death is definitely an intruder into God's world, an enemy of God and man. Our dread of death is not so much a fear of the act of dying, but a dread of shattering our familiar relationships and precious interests. Perhaps death is no more drastic than the experience of birth is for a baby when it is suddenly brought from the mother's womb into the strange environment of this world. Nevertheless, we fear it.

If our Lord tarries, we shall go the way of all the earth. These bodies of ours will die and be buried. But that is not the end. The Apostle Paul spoke this way about the body: "Sown in corruption, it is raised in incorruption. . . . Sown in dishonor, it is raised in glory. . . . Sown in weakness, it

46

is raised in power. . . . Sown a natural body, it is raised a spiritual body. . . . For the trumpet shall sound, and the dead shall be raised incorruptible, and we shall be changed. For this corruptible must put on incorruption, and this mortal must put on immortality." Then will death be swallowed up in victory, and our triumph will begin. (See 1 Cor. 15:42-44, 52-54.)

No longer hindered by the infirmities of a dying body, we shall at last be able to enter into the joys and delights of heaven. Our limitations will vanish, our wrinkles will disappear, and in the plan of God, great highways of eternal usefulness will unfold before us. Free from the sin that enslaved us in this life, we shall enter the fullness of living that God intended man to enjoy, had not sin come into the world to wreck it all. Free from the undertow of our natural body and from the assaults of Satan, we shall share the joys of an endless and a perfect life. These bodies, once changed from mortality to immortality, will never sicken or grow old.

Can this be just a dream? Can all this be idle speculation? It is the very center of the Christian message. If you take heaven out of the Bible, the rest of its message is without meaning. If you take resurrection out of Christianity, there is no hope and no victory, only the darkness of the grave.

The greatest statement in all the Bible on the subject of resurrection is to be found in Paul's first letter to the Corinthian Christians. Here in one of the most marvelous passages in all literature, Paul wrote of our ultimate triumph in life after death, linking it completely to the empty tomb and the risen Christ.

The glory of the Christian faith is that it takes in two

worlds at a time—the present one and also the life that is to come. Life is not ended here. Our guarantee of a hereafter is the resurrection of Jesus Christ.

In a superlative climax to his letter, Paul anticipated two questions of those who doubt the future life. First, "How are the dead raised up?" and second, "With what body do they come?" In the answer to these two questions lies the root of the whole matter.

How Are the Dead Raised?

What is the manner of the resurrection, and what is the method? When the body dies, it is laid in the grave. It does not lie intact until some resurrection day, but decays. It dissolves into nature and becomes dust, enriching Mother Earth.

Now in what way are the dead raised up? How is resurrection achieved? How can a body, disintegrated and dissolved, be brought back together again? As years go by, those elements are gone. Are those very same molecules to be assembled again as if some mighty magnet has drawn them? And if that were possible, would such bodies be suited for an eternal order? These molecules are material. What place could they occupy in the spiritual domain? Paul wrote to the Corinthians, "Flesh and blood cannot inherit the kingdom of God, nor does the perishable inherit the imperishable" (15:50, NIV).

It seems that the real difficulty in accepting the doctrine of the resurrection of the body lies in our assumption that future bodies are to be of the same nature as the bodies we now have—bodies of flesh and blood, nourished by food and drink and sustained by breath, and by sleep that "knits up the ravell'd sleave of care" (Shakespeare, Macbeth).

Paul called this assumption utter foolishness. He argued that there are infinite varieties here on earth. There are variations in plants and animals. "All flesh is not the same; men have one kind of flesh, animals have another, birds another, and fish another. There are also heavenly bodies and there are earthly bodies; but the splendor of the heavenly bodies is one kind, and the splendor of the earthly bodies is another" (15:39, NIV). It is plain that even the sun and the moon and the stars differ from each other in glory. Our future body will differ from our present one. The present one is corruptible and weak and natural. The changed body will be incorruptible and powerful and glorious and spiritual.

The first man, Adam, was created with a natural body fitted for an earthly life. As such, he and we are not adapted to a heavenly existence. But the Head of the new creation is Christ, "the last Adam." By His Spirit we are quickened—given a new life and changed. This is why, for believers, death has lost its sting.

For since by man came death, by man came also the resurrection of the dead. For as in Adam all die, even so in Christ shall all be made alive. . . .

The first man Adam was made a living soul; the last Adam was made a quickening spirit. . . .

The first man is of the earth, earthy; the second Man is the Lord from heaven (1 Cor. 15:21-22, 45, 47).

For if, by the trespass of the one man, death reigned through that one man, how much more will those who receive God's abundant provision of grace and of the gift of righteousness reign in life through the one Man, Jesus Christ (Rom. 5:17, NIV).

Death is an exodus, a passing from one form of existence

to another. It is not annihilation. Nor is it unconscious soul sleep. It is, for the Christian, an entering into the presence of the Lord.

Although we will all be changed, we will retain our identifiable characteristics. The disciples knew our Lord's risen body, and Moses and Elijah were recognized at the transfiguration of Christ. In our Lord's story of Dives and Lazarus (Luke 16), there was memory of the earthly life. Lazarus was still Lazarus on the other side, and the rich man was still Dives.

The Scriptures clearly show that in resurrection glory, our new bodies are identified with those we have here. The materials of which a body consists in this life change many times, yet the body is the same. Who is equal to an explanation of what constitutes identity in this life? There is more to it than the recognition of wrinkles and blemishes, warts and dental work. But when we speak of identity in the afterlife—here is something the nature of which we cannot explain until we reach the other shore. A recognition which is not primarily physical, but spiritual, beggars human thought!

The most profound fact underlying this whole argument was categorically stated by Paul, and his statement comes to the heart of the whole matter: God gives to each kind of life "a body as He has determined" (1 Cor. 15:38, NIV). It therefore depends on God's will. As a grain of wheat buried in the earth takes on a new life and is given a new body, its identity with the old is a mystery beyond our ability to analyze. By the same principle, the human body dies and rises to new life and form, for "so it will be with the resurrection of the dead. The body that is sown is perishable. It is raised imperishable . . . . It is sown a natural body, it is raised a spiritual body. If there is a natural body, there is also a spiritual body" (15:42-44, NIV).

The questions of the skeptic deserve Paul's chiding reply, "Thou fool" (v. 36), in the light of what we see going on in nature. It is as though Paul were saying, "You unperceiving man. Open your eyes. See what is going on each day around you, and you will never again be troubled with that problem; for the resurrection of the body, however mysterious it may be, is a familiar thing in the realm of nature."

Consider the miracle of the harvest. Custom has dulled its wonder. Familiarity has blunted its lesson. But look at the seed—a bare grain. You put it in the ground, and it decays; but by a divine power, it rises again, not the body you buried, but a new body, and without losing its identity. Mystery of mysteries! That new body is related to the old one, having come out of it. To say we do not believe in the harvest, because we do not understand the process, is to play the fool. We are amazed at the harvest. It is a perpetual miracle. And though we may be unequal to explain it, we must admit that the harvest brings us face to face with a sovereign God in whose mighty hand the maturing grain ripens as regularly as the seasons turn.

The miracles of God are all around us. Even in the smallest flower, there are infinite mysteries. To completely understand a flower, we would need to be as wise as God. That is something of the feeling that Tennyson had when he wrote:

Flower in the crannied wall,
I pluck you out of the crannies;
I hold you here, root and all, in my hand.

Little flower—but if I could understand
What you are, root and all, and all in all,
I should know what God and man is.

There are mysteries in this life that we cannot fully
fathom. We are equipped with a three-dimensional mind,
but God is infinite in dimension. The miracle of the harvest
is a constant witness to the power of God to translate death
into a different dimension of life. So also is the resurrection
of the dead.

Lazarus and the daughter of Jairus were restored to life
by the power of God. But they were brought back to the
same natural life, only to die again. That was not resurrection. The form of their bodies was not changed. But when
the body of Jesus came from the tomb, it was changed. And
in His resurrection we behold the "firstfruits of them that
slept" (15:20). He was the same Jesus, and yet His body
was no longer bound by the physical limitations which He
took when He humbled Himself and was made flesh. So we
will have a resurrected body—a new body given of God as
it pleases Him.

With What Body?

A new body, a changed body? Yes, but what is it like? In
deeply moving words, Paul pointed out some of the characteristics that distinguish the resurrection body from the
one in which we now live.

"It is sown in corruption. . . . raised in incorruption."
The story of every human body is that it wears out. It is
easily injured, and needs constant repairs. It is subject to
disease and death. Thus we have doctors and hospitals and
medicines. But all the nourishment and care and medical

skill in the world cannot guarantee that a man will live as long as a tree. However pompous or lavish the funeral, we have to hurry the corpse away because of corruption. In earlier generations, floral decorations at funerals were not only beautiful, but also had a practical use—they helped overcome the odor of decay!

The body of the resurrection will not be subject to corruption, from age, accident, or disease. The resurrection body will be incorruptible, free from pain, decay, and death. It will never wear out. This body will be different from anything we have known. It will never die. We shall outlive the stars!

"It is sown in dishonor . . . raised in glory" (v. 43). How repulsive is a corpse! We would not want to keep it. Custom and respect demand that we reverently dispose of it. The attractiveness of a body is short-lived. But it will be raised in glory, resplendent in brightness. That is to say, in a glorified body, made like the body of our risen Lord. "We look for the Saviour, the Lord Jesus Christ; who shall change our vile body, that it may be fashioned like unto His glorious body" (Phil. 3:20-21). In His resurrected body, Jesus surmounted the limitations of this life, passing through closed doors and barred windows and thick walls. Earth had no power to stop Him. We expect our bodies to be the same.

"It is sown in weakness . . . raised in power." We work for a few hours and quickly tire. We are aware of our physical limitations, as we cannot do all that we would. We tell ourselves that, after all, we are only human. We are disqualified from invincibility by bodily weakness.

But in heaven we will never grow weary. Power is the promise of God. We will have faculties with which we are not now acquainted, and our abilities will be enlarged. Perhaps we will possess aptitudes that are entirely new, with vistas that go far beyond the horizon of earth's limited life.

"It is sown a natural body . . . raised a spiritual body." The body that we lay in the grave is a natural body, fitted for this world and so often mastered by the feelings and the mind.

But the body of the resurrection is entirely different. Existing on a higher plane, it is spirit-governed, and no longer mastered by animal appetite. All of its appetites will be purified and refined, and in accord with the Spirit of God. For it will be adapted and fitted for heaven, our eternal home.

We know from experience what a natural body is. We dress, doctor, and care for it. But what is a spiritual body? We must never think of it as an intangible, ethereal thing. Our Lord's body after His resurrection was not wispy and transparent, but tangible. He had a material body. To Thomas He said, "Behold My hands and My feet, that it is I Myself; handle Me, and see; for a spirit hath not flesh and bones, as ye see Me have" (Luke 24:39). By the shore of the Sea of Galilee, Jesus ate bread and fish at breakfast with His disciples. He was no ghost. He was real.

Of course there are mysteries beyond our grasp. There will always be enigmas to our finite minds. But if our trust is in the risen Lord, the solution to our problem is ultimately in the revelation that God gives each one a body as it has pleased Him (1 Cor. 15:38).

"Behold," He concluded, "I show you a mystery." What is that mystery? It is simply this: "We shall all be changed" (v. 51). That is the heart of it. Life will not be as we have known it here. Something will happen, something supernatural. We shall all be changed and will enter a new order. Life will no longer be lived on this low, mortal level but on a higher, spiritual level. Recognition will be no more on the human level, but on the spiritual. Hopes and loves and desires will be no more on the earthly level, but on the spiritual, fitted for heaven, and freed from our mundane boundaries and restrictions.

With such a prospect and such a promise, there is little wonder that Christians can join the triumphant shout: "O Grave, where is thy victory?" (v. 55)

Will We Know Each Other There?

It is possible to conceive of a future life where personal identity does not exist, and where we are no longer the persons we now know ourselves to be. However, there are two strong reasons why as Christians, we believe in the existence of our personal identity after death and in our future ability to recognize that identity both in ourselves and in others. The first is in the very nature of personality. The second is in the plan of God as revealed in the Scriptures.

The Nature of Personality

In this vast universe there are no two flowers exactly alike. There are no two leaves of the forest exactly the same. There are no two stars that are identical. The Creator God favors variety. In this universe there is infinite variety and dissimilarity. Therefore, we reason that there must be a unique purpose and plan for every creature.

Far back in the plan of God, every one of us was created with a distinct and specific personality. It is a startlingly wonderful fact that in all the world no two persons are precisely alike in their bodily forms or in their natures.

You are a distinct creation. There never was another being exactly like you, and there never will be. No two people in the world have ever lived with precisely the same qualities of mind and heart, the same passions, the same loves and hates, and the same hereditary tendencies.

When genius in any sphere of life appears, we are accustomed to say, "After God made him, He broke the mold." That is to say, "He never made another like him." But that statement is also true of the commonest man.

What a mysterious and wonderful thing is this awareness of separate identity! No fainting spell or momentary unconsciousness can destroy it. No anesthetic can kill it. It survives each night of sleep. And because this identity persists and has in it the very instinct of immortality, we are deeply persuaded and convinced that even the experience of death can have no power to annihilate it. Identity must still abide and continue beyond the sunset and into the infinite life that God has provided in heaven.

The Plan of God

The second reason for our belief in personal identity and recognition after death is found in the Scriptures, where God has revealed His plan for mankind.

The writers of the Old Testament, by the inspiration of God, spoke in significant language of departing this life. For example, they said of Abraham that he "died in a good old age, an old man, and full of years; and was gathered to his people" (Gen. 25:8). The same expression was used for the deaths of Isaac (35:29) and Jacob (49:29). When Aaron, the high priest, died, he too was "gathered unto his people" (Num. 20:24). In the Book of Judges, we read of a whole new generation that died and "were gathered unto their fathers" (Jud. 2:10). All this would seem to indicate that their identity would not be lost. If it were, what would it avail them to be with their fathers or their people?

Bathsheba's first child born to David died as the Prophet Nathan had predicted. The parents were heartbroken. In the agony of his loss, David cried, "I shall go to him, but he shall not return to me" (2 Sam. 12:23). Surely, there is no meaning in this statement unless there will one day be a glorious reunion and recognition.

In the New Testament, we see an ever clearer picture, in Christ's story of Dives and Lazarus. On the other side, the beggar Lazarus recognized himself as Lazarus. Dives recognized himself as Dives, and spoke of himself as "I." Furthermore, each recognized the other and remembered what took place on earth. Each connected his identity there with his identity here. Dives remembered five brothers that he had left behind. In no sense was identity blurred.

There are those who say that this story (Luke 16) is a parable and is not to be taken as an historical record. Even if that were so, the teaching is there and cannot be denied. Jesus pictured the hereafter as a place of recognition, both in heaven and beyond the great gulf in hades.

Jesus explained to His disciples that His Jewish rejecters, the privileged children of the kingdom, would be cast into outer darkness, while many outsiders from the east and west would sit down with Abraham, Isaac, and Jacob in that new life and that eternal fellowship. (See Matt. 8:11-

12.) But what would be the significance of that if we would not recognize them?

Our Lord's words to the repentant thief on the cross suggested the same prospect of identity: "Today shalt thou be with Me in paradise" (Luke 23:43).

There is a great passage about personal immortality that our Lord quoted from the Old Testament. Long after Abraham, Isaac, and Jacob were dead, God had said to Moses, "I am the God of thy father, the God of Abraham, the God of Isaac, and the God of Jacob" (Ex. 3:6). To His retelling of this, Jesus added a forceful word: "God is not the God of the dead, but of the living" (Matt. 22:32). By this He clearly implied that these three patriarchs were still alive in their identities as Abraham, Isaac, and Jacob, and that He still had dealings with them as He did on earth.

On the mountain of the Transfiguration, Moses and Elijah appeared with Jesus. Their topic of conversation was His approaching death which He was about to accomplish at Jerusalem. Moses and Elijah were recognized by Jesus. In some way they seem also to have been recognized by Peter, James, and John. It may be that Jesus identified them. The point is, however, that they had kept their identities.

The Significance of Identity

If there is a survival of personal identity, several inescapable conclusions are obvious.

• It is clear that we can never get away from ourselves. All that we have in this world, we leave behind us; but all that we are, we take with us into the life beyond. We cannot slip away from what we are and begin over again. We cannot shake ourselves off like that. Perhaps it was that inescapability from our personalities that made John say, "He that is unjust, let him be unjust still; and he which is filthy, let him be filthy still; and he that is righteous, let him be righteous still; and he that is holy, let him be holy still" (Rev. 22:11). What we are will remain.

• Since personal identity is not lost, it is logical to believe that we shall know our friends in heaven. We have little trouble recognizing them in this world. Why would we conceive of a heaven where we are more limited than here? Such a reply is not flippant. It is good common sense. We are going there with all our faculties about us. We are not going into a mist of vague fancies, a lotus land where nothing is real or recognized. Heaven is no dream. It is a place, real, practical, and as sure as Almighty God Himself.

• The third conclusion to which we are driven is that every individual soul is of infinite value to God and has its own special place in His scheme of things. The more deeply we look into the plan of redemption, the more we see that it revolves around the individual soul. The personality is precious. God's purpose in a world developed through long ages is that it should be a platform for this personal "I" to grow and develop. We are of such value to our Creator that He gave His only begotten Son to redeem the immortal "I." The present intercession of Jesus, the fellowship assured, and the mansions prepared are to provide a background for the growth of that mysterious "I."

• And last of all, if personal identity survives death, it is clear that the Christian is in Christ, that he lives with Christ, and that death cannot alter this relationship which is his through the gift of faith.

The fact is that the dead in Christ are closer than ever to Him. Being with Christ after death is a higher order of eternal life than being with Him here and now. It is a long step nearer the final goal when the company of the redeemed will be complete. That is why Paul could say it is "far better."

7

What Are the Resources of Heaven?

In picturing the new dimensions of heaven and contrasting them with our life on earth, the Bible is both negative and positive. We know that in heaven there will be no more pain or sorrow or curse of sin. There will be no tears, no night, no need of the sun, no more sea. Heaven will be glorious because of the things that are *not* there. But heaven will also be beautiful because of the things that *are* there. To complete the picture, let us consider both.

No Sin in Heaven

We are part of a fallen race, and the blight of sin has damaged every phase of life. We have inherited a sin nature; in human experience all have sinned and come short of the glory of God. In Christ we are regenerated and given a new nature. Judicially, the old sin nature, the guilt of our sinful acts, and the imputed guilt of Adam's first sin are blotted out.

But even as Christians we have a constant warfare going between what we were in Adam and what we are in Christ. Paul referred to it as the struggle between the old man and the new man. Summing up this battle he said, "I find then a law, that when I would do good, evil is present with me" (Rom. 7:21). But in heaven there is no sin. It is banished. It is blotted out through the redemption provided by Jesus Christ.

In Revelation 22:3 we read, "And there shall be no more curse." Because of Adam's sin, a curse was put upon all creation (Gen. 3:17-19). But in heaven there shall be no more curse. How different life will be without sin! In this life we are shocked each day with the tale of it. There are derelictions and crimes in high places and in low. Some of them make the story of Sodom seem like a Sunday School picnic. "The heart is deceitful above all things, and desperately wicked; who can know it?" (Jer. 17:9) Wherever we turn we are face to face with stealing, lying, deception, adultery, fornication, murders—crime in its every form. Even those who deny the reality of sin, and who excuse it as growing pains, are not willing to take the locks off their doors or dismiss the police force! But in heaven these foul stains will be gone, "and there shall in no wise enter into it anything that defileth, neither whatsoever worketh abomination, or maketh a lie" (Rev. 21:27).

Heaven is, therefore, a holy place. Satan, the prince of darkness, will no longer contest every inch with the Lord of Light and Life. In that land fairer than day, no evil shall ever enter. We will not only see Christ, but we shall be like Him.

No Tears, Pain, or Death in Heaven

There will be no tears in heaven. Twice in the description of the Christian's life after death, we are told that God shall wipe away all tears (Rev. 7:17; 21:4). We all have learned that happiness unalloyed cannot be found on this earth. Tears are the evidence of unhappiness and sorrow, but in that day there will be no more sorrow.

Our resurrection bodies will also be free from disease and sickness and the pain that attends them. These resulted from the fall of man, and virtually none of us escapes. And for some, the disease is so agonizing, so awful, that they cry out for death. But in the land above, aches and pains will be no more. Neither will there be mental or spiritual anguish, for all doubt and fear will have vanished and the pangs of remorse will be fully gone.

Since heaven is a place of joy in its fullness, there will be no grief. There will be no death, for our last great enemy is conquered and the sadness of final farewell is unknown. Death came by sin, but with sin and Satan out of the way, our problems are over, and the life is eternal. The funeral bell that tolled for all is at last silent. Upon our heads is the crown of life. "And God shall wipe away all tears from [our] eyes; and there shall be no more death, neither sorrow, nor crying, neither shall there be any more pain; for the former things are passed away" (Rev. 21:4).

No Separation in Heaven

We read of a new heaven and a new earth where there is no more sea (Rev. 21:1). Certainly, this is not written to tell us about the geography of a future world. Rather, it is a symbol, the embodiment of a great spiritual truth. What is meant by this symbol is best understood by remembering how the sea appeared to the Jew. The Jew was not a sailor. The references to the sea in the Old Testament were not from the point of view of a lover of the sea, but rather from one who feared it. In Jewish eyes the sea was a haunting thing, speaking of separation and mystery and restlessness. For all eternity we will dwell together with the Lord and His redeemed ones. And there will be no separation—and the heartache that attends it—from loved ones who live beyond the broad horizon.

That is why John rejoiced to announce that in heaven there will be no more sea. No more mystery, no more separation, no more restlessness of turbulent waters. There is going to be an end to that someday. One of our favorite figures of speech describes life as a voyage over a stormy sea with raging waves and treacherous shoals, but that is going to end someday. The disquiet and unrest, the chaos of changing circumstances, and the stormy billows known to us all in this life will be no more.

But all this is negative. Heaven is wonderful because of the things that are not there. But heaven is far more wonderful because of what we shall find there. This is the positive picture.

Two great factors enter into the life of heaven. They are the two important factors on which our happiness is chiefly based here. The first is fellowship, and the second is service. In eternal love and eternal labor, life finds its perfection.

Fellowship in Heaven

Every true conception of heaven makes much of fellowship. The writer of the Book of Hebrews contrasted Israel's coming to Sinai with our coming to the heavenly city, the New Jerusalem, to the general assembly of the firstborn.

Ye are not come unto the mount that might be touched, and that burned with fire, nor unto blackness and darkness and tempest. . . . But ye are come unto Mount Sion, and unto the city of the living God, the heavenly Jerusalem, and to an innumerable company of angels, to the general assembly and church of the firstborn, which are written in heaven, and to God the Judge of all, and to the spirits of just men made perfect, and to Jesus the Mediator of the New Covenant (Heb. 12:18, 22-24).

We look forward to the company of justified saints made mature and perfect in the faith and in the communion of saints. In this nobility of heaven, there is a fellowship of saints in which everyone will feel at home and where mind and soul will find fullest expression and expansion and fondest delight.

There will be the fellowship of our own dear ones who went through death's gate before us and await our coming. There can be nothing more sure than that the Bible's picture of the Father's house is one of true fellowship. The conventional relationships, the racial affinities, the national ties, the family connections will disappear, and the spiritual kinships alone will predominate.

Jesus taught that there would be no marriage in heaven and no childbearing. The creation of life will have ended. We invariably ask if the human ties here will obtain in heaven. His disciples asked this question of our Lord, and His answer was that in the resurrection, "they neither marry, nor are given in marriage, but are as the angels which are in heaven" (Mark 12:25). The answer to the question about continuity of human relationships is that if the ties are spiritual, they will abide in the life beyond.

The supreme fellowship in heaven will be the fellowship

with our Lord. That will be the glory of our future life. There is a world of truth in Charles Gabriel's well-loved song:

> When all my labors and trials are o'er,
> And I am safe on that beautiful shore,
> Just to be near the dear Lord I adore
> Will through the ages be glory for me.

The central glory of heaven is Christ. To have walked and talked with Him, as the disciples did, must have been a great privilege; but it is nothing compared with what lies ahead for those who are redeemed. "Father, I will that they also, whom Thou hast given Me, be with Me where I am; that they may behold My glory" (John 17:24). Paul was convinced that to depart and be with Christ was far better. He thrilled at the thought of that great day. And we too shall come to it, as surely as God has promised.

Service in Heaven

The second outstanding feature of the heavenly life is service. Many think of heaven as rest. It is a natural thought, especially for those who are overworked and heavily burdened. To such Jesus said, "Come unto Me . . . and I will give you rest" (Matt. 11:28). It was the Apostle John who on Patmos heard a voice from heaven saying, "Write, 'Blessed are the dead which die in the Lord from henceforth;' 'Yea,' saith the Spirit, 'that they may rest from their labors; and their works do follow them'" (Rev. 14:13).

But is it not true that the unhappiest people and the most restless are the unemployed? The truest form of rest is not inactivity but joyous work and welcome service.

"They rest from their labors." Certainly! From unwelcome toil and heavy burdens. Yes! Deep down in all of us is the hope to one day be rid of burdensome toil. But we never hope to lounge around for eternity in a vacuum.

In his description of the throne of the Lamb of God, John wrote, "The throne of God and of the Lamb shall be in [the heavenly city], and His servants shall serve Him" (Rev. 22:3). Again we read about the white-robed saints, whose robes are made white by the blood of the Lamb, and who serve Him day and night in His temple. (See Rev. 7:13-15.) There will be activity in heaven, and that activity will be true service. Perhaps the best way to comprehend this is to say that heaven is a place of work, but without the curse of toil.

There are two things against which every normal soul revolts. One is work that is uncongenial; the other is idleness. When work becomes a burden, it is usually because it is uncongenial. Perhaps a disagreement with management, or a displeasing circumstance that makes compatibility impossible turns the work into a drudgery. But the work that awaits us in heaven will be a delight to the soul. We will not weary of it. Perhaps that is what Rudyard Kipling meant when he wrote:

> When earth's last picture is painted
> And the tubes are twisted and dried,
> When the oldest colours have faded
> And the youngest critic has died,
> We shall rest, and faith, we shall need it—
> Lay down for an aeon or two,
> Till the Master of All Good Workmen
> Shall put us to work anew.

In this life we think of service in terms of helpfulness to others. Even when we speak of serving the Lord, we have in mind caring for the less fortunate, about whom Jesus said, "Inasmuch as ye have done it unto one of the least of these My brethren, ye have done it unto Me" (Matt. 25:40).

But in heaven we are not ministering in Christ's name to needy or suffering souls. "His servants shall serve Him" (Rev. 22:3). How shall we serve Him? The words of this text are remarkable in that the Greek words for *servant* and *serve* are not related to one another as they are in the English language. The word *servant* means literally "a slave," but the word *serve* is in Scripture reserved for one kind of service—the service of worship. It has to do with the activity of the priest in the temple, and could never be used for any good turn we might do for man. It is exclusively a word for the temple, referring to an activity which is all worship and is directed to the Lamb of God upon His throne. In most of the new versions of the Bible this difference is noted, and the text reads, "His servants shall worship Him."

The rabbis taught that there are angels who serve and angels who praise, as though these were two separate functions; but at the throne of God, these two are one. The Martha and the Mary of our Christian experience shall be blended together in such a way that our service shall be praise, and our praise shall be service.

Are There Rewards in Heaven?

The last book of the Bible closes with words from the One who declares Himself to be Alpha and Omega, the first and the last. "And, behold, I come quickly; and My reward is with Me, to give every man according as his work shall be" (Rev. 22:12). Jesus admonished His disciples to deny self and take up the cross, saying, "For the Son of man shall come in the glory of His Father with His angels; and then He shall reward every man according to his works" (Matt. 16:27).

Candy for Goodness?

In our day we encounter quibbling pedantics who deplore the idea of heaven as a place for rewards. They regard the promise of reward as a low and carnal incentive to righteousness, entirely unworthy of a mature person. They liken it to offering candy to a child if he will be good, and they view this as inferior strategy.

his judgment parable, as he pictured the Judgment Seat of Christ. (See 1 Cor. 3.) All who are redeemed by the blood shed on Calvary's cross will stand before the Judgment Seat of Christ.

We must all appear before the Judgment Seat of Christ; that everyone may receive the things done in his body, according to that he hath done, whether it be good or bad (2 Cor. 5:10).

For we shall all stand before the Judgment Seat of Christ (Rom. 14:10).

Be not deceived; God is not mocked; for whatsoever a man soweth, that shall he also reap (Gal. 6:7).

And whatsoever you do, do it heartily, as to the Lord and not unto men; knowing that of the Lord you shall receive the reward of the inheritance; for you serve the Lord Christ. But he that doeth wrong shall receive for the wrong which he hath done; and there is no respect of persons (Col. 3:23-25).

These verses make it plain that our deeds will face us at the Judgment Seat of Christ. All the dishonesty and impurity and gossip and slander and malice, and all the works of the flesh, hidden perhaps now, will be opened in heaven and will determine the reward or the loss to the believer.

Rewards for Service

We have assurance from Christ Himself that, "He that heareth My word, and believeth on Him that sent Me, hath everlasting life, and shall not come into condemnation; but is passed from death unto life" (John 5:24). And Paul comforted all Christians in these great words: "There is, therefore, now no condemnation to them which are in Christ Jesus" (Rom. 8:1). There is no judgment for God's

One answer from those skies is sent,
"Ye who from God depart
While it is called today, repent
And harden not your heart."

—Author unknown

The only solution to our sin problem is to be found in the Gospel as the apostles preached it. The key is repentance toward God and faith in His Son, Jesus Christ. This faith is the only rock on which our house may stand. The voices of patriarchs, prophets, apostles, and preachers join in the great invitation: "Seek you the Lord while He may be found; call you upon Him while He is near" (Isa. 55:6).

hearts, we will understand how it is possible to be on the right Foundation and yet build with wood, hay, and stubble.

Gold, silver, and precious stones—what do they mean? They are symbols of sincere living and sacrificial serving. They are tokens of true stewardship and self-denial, of practical kindness and Christlike love. They are the solid truths of the Christian life put into practice. If our faith is doing nothing but comforting us in the belief that we will escape the horrors of hell, it is really no faith at all, for "faith without works is dead" (James 2:20). It is sadly possible to be very busy building layers of good, intermixed with layers of bad.

Every man's work shall be made manifest, for the day shall declare it. Payday someday! The day is, of course, the day of His coming. The purging, testing fire of divine approval will reveal the true value of his work. And the fire shall try every man's work, of what sort it is. It is not how much his work is, but of what sort.

Here is a searching word—the motive of our work is what counts. In that day God will test everything by His standard of truth, and if it meets with His approval, a reward will be given. This reward is not salvation, for salvation is of grace, altogether apart from works (Eph. 2:8-9). But this reward is for faithful service, because of salvation.

No One Is Exempt

So then it comes to this—for Christians on the true Foundation, there will come a day of judgment and testing of the real value of life's work. None are exempt, for judgment will begin at the house of God. In that day some works will be consumed as by fire because they are worthless, but some will be immortal; and like gold, silver, and precious stones, they will stand the test.

But what of the outcome of the two sorts of material used in the building? One man is rewarded; the other is not. Instead, he suffers loss. He has not lost his salvation. He is still on the Foundation, but he is saved, "so as by fire" (1 Cor. 3:15). Yes, he will get through, because, in spite of his worldliness and the worthlessness of his labors, he had a feeble faith in Jesus Christ.

Evidently, some will enjoy an abundant entrance into the land of glory, while others just make it by the skin of their teeth! (See 2 Peter 1:10-11.) Evidently, there are degrees of reward in heaven just as there are degrees of punishment in hell. The warning of this judgment parable gives meaning to the song:

> Must I go, and empty-handed
> Must I meet my Saviour so?
> Not one soul with which to greet Him:
> Must I empty-handed go?

A day is coming when the worth of individual service for Christ will be tested for what it is. That work which abides will be rewarded, and that which is burned up will mean a great loss to the careless builder.

We attach great importance to last sayings, and we linger lovingly over final farewells. The greatest giant Rome ever had within her prison walls was the Apostle Paul. Nero had signed his death warrant. The only question was, When?

Paul wrote these final words to young Timothy, his son in Christ! "I am now ready to be offered, and the time of my departure is at hand. I have fought a good fight; I have finished my course; I have kept the faith. Henceforth there is laid up for me a crown of righteousness which the Lord, the righteous Judge, will give me at that day; and not to me only, but unto all them that love His appearing" (2 Tim. 4:6-8).

They led the apostle outside the city and along the road to the place of execution, and the headsman was ready. Paul knelt beside the block. "For to me to live is Christ," he had said, "and to die is gain" (Phil. 1:21). There was the flash of the mattock. The fight was over; the race was run—the crown at last. "Well done . . . enter thou into the joy of thy Lord" (Matt. 25:21).

Our turn will come one day. If we see that possibility from where we are, let us redouble our efforts. Let us cling to the trust that is committed to us, for the Lord is about to appear, and He expects that we shall have held the faith undiminished and undefiled.

"Look to yourselves, that we lose not those things which we have wrought, but that we receive a full reward" (2 John 8).

"Let no man beguile you of your reward" (Col. 2:18).

"Hold that fast . . . that no man take thy crown" (Rev. 3:11). Five crowns are mentioned in the Bible. Perhaps a crown is a human way of saying we will receive a reward and hear those words: "Well done, thou good and faithful servant."

Payday Someday— Is There a Reckoning Day?

Out of the moral makeup of human nature, there arises a fundamental and unshakable conviction that there will be a day of reckoning when "there is nothing covered, that shall not be revealed; and hid, that shall not be known" (Matt. 10:26). That is an instinct in us similar to the instinct of immortality.

On the walls of tombs in ancient Egypt, the judgment of the dead is depicted. Scales are painted containing, on one side of the balance, the soul of man and on the other, the symbol of truth; and a priest is marking down the verdict.

The latent sense of justice deep down in the heart of man cries out for a time when all wrongs will be punished and all virtues rewarded.

The Bible on Judgment
The idea of a future judgment was not invented by Christianity; but like immortality, it has been brought to light in

the unveiling of the Gospel.

No one can read the New Testament without discovering how this truth of judgment is made to stand out on the plan of the ages. Hear these words!

It is appointed unto men once to die, but after this the judgment (Heb. 9:27).

He hath appointed a day, in the which He will judge the world in righteousness by that Man whom He hath ordained (Acts 17:31).

We must all appear before the Judgment Seat of Christ; that everyone may receive the things done in his body; according to that he hath done, whether it be good or bad (2 Cor. 5:10).

And I saw the dead, small and great, stand before God; and the books were opened . . . and the dead were judged . . . according to their works. And the sea gave up the dead which were in it, and death and hell delivered up the dead which were in them; and they were judged every man according to their works (Rev. 20:12-13).

These words ought to convince us beyond any shadow of doubt that we are heading toward a great court of divine justice where the secrets of men will be made known.

It is not our purpose to discuss the various phases of God's judgment, whether for nations, believers, or unbelievers. That is a subject in itself. The purpose here is only to emphasize the fact of it.

Also, let us not confuse the righteous judgment of God in the world's history with the final assize. God does judge the world, as the psalmist says, "by terrible things in righteousness" (Ps. 65:5). He judged it in a great flood in the days of Noah. He judged it again at the Tower of Babel. In the time of the Judges, there was a constantly recurring theme of rebellion, retribution, repentance, and restoration. In the shadow of every great war or national calamity, we think we can discern the figure of the Judge Himself!

But these are not the only judgments in this life, and to suppose that they all end here would be foolish.

Paul's Sermon on Judgment

Paul's sermon on Mars Hill in Athens is a model for good preaching. After a few conciliatory remarks to gain the attention of the Athenians, he launched a blow at idolatry.

Then Paul spoke of the divine purpose in all the tangled web of history; but that great purpose has not been realized. He then spoke of the universality of sin and a universal judgment, the principle of which was rigid righteousness: "He will judge the world in righteousness by that Man whom He hath ordained; whereof He hath given assurance unto all men, in that He hath raised Him from the dead" (Acts 17:31).

Paul was saying that the resurrection of Christ is the assurance of judgment. Paul's hearers had a very shadowy belief in a future life. In their vague thinking, dismembered spirits wandered, ghostlike, in a phantom underworld. It is only the resurrection of Christ that gives meaning to the question of immortality. The resurrection of Christ, argued Paul, gives assurance to all men that the world will be judged by Jesus Himself.

There are five things about the judgment day that are set forth in this sermon. First, the certainty of it; second, the universality of it; third, the basis of it; fourth, the Administrator of it; and fifth, the issues of it.

1. The certainty. God "hath appointed a day in the

which He will judge the world in righteousness" (Acts 17:31). The statement is clean and simple. The person who lives in sin may laugh at it, but he cannot laugh it away. In the days of Noah, men laughed, but the Flood came. In the days of Lot, they laughed, but judgment fell on them. In the days of Jeremiah, they laughed at the predictions about Nebuchadnezzar and the fall of Judah, but they happened. In Christ's day, they laughed at His prediction concerning the destruction of Jerusalem by Titus (A.D. 70), but it took place and there was left not one stone upon another.

All of God's predictions about judgment on individuals and on nations past have come true to the very letter. If we are to judge the future by the past—and there is no other way to do it—God's words about future judgments will come true, to the very letter.

Just as surely as God raised Jesus from the dead, there will be a judgment day. It is right and it is reasonable. It is the law of moral gravity. The resurrection of Jesus is the special guarantee of judgment; and since that resurrection is not fiction but a part of history, we may be assured that the judgment is real and that it is certain.

The names Littleton and West were once famous in legal circles, for they were eminent lawyers. In religion they claimed to be deists, a title which at that time designated anyone who believed in a divinity. It was used as the opposite of *atheist*. However, they did not believe that God revealed Himself; and they therefore rejected the doctrine of the Trinity. They had no room for Christ, the supernatural, or the hereafter.

One day in conversation, they agreed that they could not maintain their deistic position unless they could dispose of two things. The first was the reputed resurrection of Jesus

Christ from the dead, and the second was the reputed conversion of Saul of Tarsus.

Littleton said he would like to research the matter of Saul's so-called conversion and write a book to disprove it. West agreed that he would do the same with the story of the resurrection of Christ.

After thorough research, they wrote their books. Later when they met, West said to Littleton, "How have you fared in your work?"

"I have studied it," said Littleton, "from a legal standpoint, and I have become convinced that Saul was, indeed, converted; and I have become a Christian. How is it with you?"

"Well," said West, "I have sifted all the evidence for the Resurrection, and I am satisfied that Jesus of Nazareth was raised from the dead just as the Bible claims He was. And I have, therefore, written my book in defense of Christianity" (*Encyclopedia Britannica*, Vol. 17, p. 185).

It is difficult for a man with legal training, accustomed to sifting the evidence, to thoroughly investigate the evidence for the Resurrection, and still deny that Jesus rose. And Paul in his Mars Hill sermon claimed Christ's resurrection as the guarantee that God had appointed a day in which He will judge the world in righteousness.

2. *The universality*. The second thing made clear about judgment is the universality of it. God hath "appointed a day in the which He will judge *the world*." This is not a class judgment. This is not judgment of a nation or a family. Every man and woman who has ever lived will be judged individually. A person often escapes justice here. Many a criminal has never been arrested, and remains at large. But when God sends forth His detectives for that judgment

day, they will find everyone.

3. The basis. The judgment will be based on the deeds done in the body (2 Cor. 5:10). That person who is living in sin, dissipation, debauchery, and immorality will have to answer for it. Also, that one who is making gold his god; and the person who knows the truth but will not obey it. That businessman who knows the right path but will not follow it, because it might hurt his business or damage him in society, will answer. As will the libertine living in lust. The deeds done in the body—yes, they will all come up. Secret sins will be open in heaven (Rom. 2:16).

Even our words will one day be judged (Matt. 12:36). Our studied speeches do not reveal what we really are, but our idle words do. They are careless and sometimes thoughtless. They drop accidentally, and too often they are impure and vulgar.

Since God has sent His Son into the world to be our Saviour, the deliberate rejection of Him is the most damning sin of all. Nothing reveals the human heart so clearly as what we do with Christ. The ultimate question on judgment day will be, "What have you done with Jesus?"

4. The Administrator. The fourth thing about the judgment day set forth in this great text is the picture of the Judge Himself. Who is to be the Judge? It is Jesus Christ Himself, our risen Lord: "That Man whom He hath ordained, whereof He hath given assurance to all men, in that He hath raised Him from the dead" (Acts 17:31). That same Christ who was rejected of men and whose word men trample underfoot is to be the Judge.

5. The issues. The eternal issues of judgment will determine destiny. They will be just and righteous in accordance with the holy attributes of God. For God has appointed a

Man who "will judge the world in righteousness" (17:31).

Faith in Jesus as our Saviour is the only way to be assured that we shall not come into judgment, but have passed from death unto life (John 5:24). Christ took our judgment for sins and paid its awful penalty. Our faith in what He has done is the root out of which will grow the full tree, bearing good fruit, resulting in "our love made perfect, that we may have boldness in the day of judgment" (1 John 4:17).

Is There a Second Chance for Heaven?

Will there be an opportunity for repentance and salvation after death? This is no idle question, for the answer makes the ultimate difference for many people. It is a question that has troubled the minds of great thinkers, for it involves the highest interests of the soul.

Alfred Lord Tennyson cherished the faith that ultimately all mankind would be redeemed and that God would at last conquer all evil. To deny this, he thought, was to admit that God in some cases would be defeated. This is how he put it:

> . . . not one life shall be destroyed,
> Or cast as rubbish to the void,
> When God has made His pile complete.

This total inclusion is comforting to many and strongly appeals to people who manufacture their own religion, rather than relying on that which is revealed. Referred to as "the larger hope," this belief is well named, because it is at best only a hope.

It is our loving Saviour who told us that the broad way leads to destruction. He who loved us enough to give Himself for us warns that sin's consequence is the worm that dieth not and the fire that is not quenched. (See Mark 9:44.)

When Dr. Samuel Johnson, great 18th-century Englishman of letters, was despondent about his eternal destiny, a Mrs. Adams said to him, "You seem, Sir, to forget the merits of our Redeemer."

"Madam," replied Johnson, "I do not forget the merits of my Redeemer; but my Redeemer has said that He will set some on His right hand and some on His left" (*Many Mansions*).

Our answer to this question of a second chance for salvation must not be based on sentiment or sympathy. To follow our natural emotions is dangerous. Therefore, in seeking a solution we must tread the sure and solid ground of scriptural revelation.

Will there be an opportunity to receive salvation in the hereafter, if a person has rejected it here? Is there a second chance? The very question narrows the field of our study. To speak of a second chance in the life to come implies that there has been a first chance in this life. The fact is, there are vast numbers of human beings who have never had a first chance to receive Christ. For example, an untold number of children have died in infancy, not yet able to discern the right hand from the left, and from whom no personal choice could be possible.

And what about those who from birth have been victims

of abnormalities? Some have had minds clouded in imbecility from the dawn of their lives. To them an intelligent choice has never been possible. They appear to be beyond what we have regarded as "the means of grace." Will they be thrust into the "outer darkness"?

When we consider that every soul is of infinite worth in the sight of God, it is impossible to believe that those who have died in infancy or without the capacity of choice are snuffed out because they are of Adam's family. We believe that for all such, full provision is made in the great redemption which Christ made possible on Calvary. The basis for their salvation is not that they were sweet and innocent and had not yet experienced sin. It is rather that the sacrifice of our Saviour on the cross is sufficient for their deliverance from the sin nature and the imputed guilt of Adam's first sin. In God's eternal mercy, it is not the will of the Father in heaven that one of these little ones should perish (Matt. 18:14).

The exceptions we have referred to only serve to focus the question the more on ourselves because we have had our first chance. All along life's way we are always having our first chance. In one way or another God is offering man his chance, but in many lives that chance is thrown away. It may be through blindness or neglect or ignorance or proud willfulness that these people reject the Saviour; but like Pharaoh they harden their hearts until the battle of the soul is lost forever. To be sure, there are many eleventh-hour repentances, but so far as we can judge, multitudes are apparently impenitent to the last, venturing out into the mystery of eternity without hope and without God.

This is why so many loved ones have wistfully asked, "Will there be another chance beyond death?" We like to think that since God is good, the way may be wider than we suppose.

The disciples experienced this quandary when they asked Jesus, "'Lord, are there few that be saved?' And He said unto them, 'Strive to enter in at the narrow gate; for many, I say unto you, will seek to enter in, and shall not be able'" (Luke 13:23-24).

Tennyson expressed that same painful question in his "In Memoriam:"

> I falter where I firmly trod
> And falling with my weight of cares
> Upon the great world's altar stairs
> That slope through darkness up to God.
>
> I stretch lame hands of faith, and grope
> And gather dust and chaff, and call
> To what I feel is "Lord of all,"
> And faintly trust the larger hope.

Yes, it is a "larger hope," but only a hope, pleasant to believe but certainly not supported by Scripture and the message of Christ Himself.

To the question of the destiny of those who die rejecting Christ, three main solutions have been offered in place of the biblical doctrine of salvation. They are Universalism, Annihilationism, and Probationism.

Universalism

The universalist claims that though all men are lost in sin, the saving work of Christ at the cross assures that all will ultimately be saved. Somehow, somewhere, sometime, God, who is not willing that any should perish, will bring about "the final harmony of all souls," and everybody will eventually be reconciled to Him. The universalist contends that the divine purpose of love cannot be defeated. It will ultimately prevail.

The basis for this is to be found in such words as, "God so loved the world that He gave His only begotten Son." The universalist seems blind to the rest of the verse, "that whosoever believeth in Him should not perish" (John 3:16). Then there are the verses, "I, if I be lifted up from the earth, will draw all men unto Me" (John 12:32). "God was in Christ reconciling the world unto Himself" (2 Cor. 5:19). Every knee shall bow and every tongue "confess that Jesus Christ is Lord" (Phil. 2:10-11).

The restitutionist goes even further, saying that eventually even the fallen angels and Satan himself will be restored, after God has made His purpose complete. He claims that this is what is taught in Acts 3:21 where Peter, speaking of Christ, said, "Whom the heaven must receive until the times of restitution of all things, which God hath spoken by the mouth of all His holy prophets since the world began."

By quoting verses out of context, it is possible to prove anything. Forcing the words of Scripture to teach what they are not intended to teach is a dangerous business!

It is true that God loved the world—the whole world. It is true that God was in Christ reconciling the world unto Himself. But it is equally true that many have not responded to His love, and that some never will. It is by no means valid to give to reason or sentiment the highest authority in these matters. So long as Scripture has a voice in our decision, utterances such as the words of Jesus concerning the sin against the Holy Spirit tip the scales against universalism. "Whosoever speaketh a word against the Son of man, it shall be forgiven him; but whosoever speaketh against the Holy Ghost, it shall not be forgiven him, neither in this world, neither in the world to come" (Matt. 12:32).

Concerning the judgment of nations spoken of by our Lord in Matthew 25:32-46, the punishment is everlasting: "Depart from Me, you cursed, into everlasting fire, prepared for the devil and his angels. . . . And these shall go away into everlasting punishment, but the righteous into life eternal" (vv. 41, 46).

With these and many other Scriptures in view, we must bow before the written Word of Him who cannot lie. It is dangerous to wish to be wiser, more merciful, and more just than our infinite Saviour Himself. The very freedom of the will, conferred on us by God in Creation, involves in itself the terrible possibility of endless resistance to our Creator and also of endless punishment.

Do you stumble at the problem of how a loving God could bring into existence a creature who would be forever shut out from Him? Then you face a similar mystery when you consider that under the government of an almighty and a holy God, sin and death could come into His perfect creation and reign from Adam until our day. Men may call universalism the "larger hope," but that does not give them the right to proclaim such hope in opposition to the teachings of Jesus, the Christ. The fact is that we have no right to teach any doctrines about God but those revealed by Himself.

Annihilationism
The annihilationist believes that those who do not repent will cease to exist at the time of death. Religious

11

What Is the Final Issue of Evil?

The primary doctrine of the resurrection speaks to the Christian's hope of eternal life. But what of those who are unrepentant to the very end and finally and irrevocably reject God's love in Jesus Christ? What does the future hold for them?

There are passages of Scripture that speak of another resurrection, which our Lord called "the resurrection of damnation." Speaking of future judgment, Jesus said, "The hour is coming, in which all that are in the graves shall hear His voice, and shall come forth; they that have done good unto the resurrection of life; and they that have done evil unto the resurrection of damnation" (John 5:28-29). In some of the newer versions, *condemnation* is used in place of *damnation*, and in others *judgment*. The Prophet Daniel saw these two destinies and wrote, "Many of them that sleep in the dust of the earth shall awake, some to everlasting life, and some to shame and everlasting contempt"

95

(Dan. 12:2).

Paul gave no support to the common idea of a general resurrection and a general judgment. His use of the word *resurrection* means "to be risen with Christ" (Col. 3:1). But other Scriptures indicate that there are two resurrections; the first for God's children at His appearing (Rev. 20:5-6), and the second for judgment of unbelievers at the Great White Throne (20:12-15). We have clues about the Christian's resurrection body, but no clues as to the form or manner of a resurrection for those who are not in Christ, and therefore not destined to eternal life.

Many people believe that death means annihilation. They seem to say that death is not too hard to face and is perhaps preferable to the struggle of life. Some people twist biblical teachings to say that unbelievers will finally be brought to a state of nothingness. In other words, they will cease to be. Hamlet called this nonbeing "a consummation devoutly to be wished." However, those who thus persuade themselves are not dealing with facts or logic.

What Is Hell?

The plain teaching of Scripture is that there are people who involve themselves in everlasting punishment by their own decisions to close their hearts finally and irrevocably to God. In the Bible such a state of punishment is called *hell*. Hell is not the invention of Paul or of the early church. We hear more about hell from the lips of the Saviour, who loved us and gave Himself for us, than we do from any of the apostles. And yet His were the gentlest lips that ever breathed the message of God's love to men. So the reality of hell is something we cannot and dare not deny. Sin is an infinitely serious matter that brought Jesus Christ to the cross, and must have dreadful consequences. Punishment in the afterlife, as well as in this life, is essential if sinners are to be brought to realize what their rebellion has meant to God, as they have spurned His love and thwarted His purpose.

Today, many people laugh at the idea of hell or just deny it. But the Bible teaches hell as a reality that Christ believed. The Apostle John wrote of Christ treading the winepress of the fierceness of the wrath of God (Rev. 19:15). Paul spoke of the "day of wrath and revelation of the righteous judgment of God, who will render to every man according to his deeds; to them who by patient continuance in well-doing seek for glory and honor and immortality, eternal life. But unto them that are contentious and do not obey the truth, but obey unrighteousness, indignation and wrath, tribulation and anguish, upon every soul of man that doeth evil" (Rom. 2:5-9).

It would be comfortable to be a universalist and tell people that they may do as they please and in the end go to heaven because of God's love. But to do so would be to ignore God's holiness and His righteousness.

Belief in hell is not completely gone except where belief in any future life is gone. It may be true that few believe in the hell of Dante's inferno or Dore's paintings. But among the greatest, safest, and sanest thinkers, there is a sure belief in a future state of woe. The moral construction of the world makes it well nigh impossible to believe otherwise. Punishment is the natural consequence of sin. There is a moral as well as a physical gravity in the universe. The law of moral gravity is expressed simply in the words, "Whatsoever a man soweth, that shall he also reap" (Gal. 6:7). Vice and virtue cannot have the same reward. If wickedness goes unpunished, there is no moral code and no reasonable justice in the universe.

Failure to recognize the difference between good and evil is philosophically absurd. And it is ethically absurd to reject the law of harvest which says: "He that soweth to his flesh shall of the flesh reap corruption; but he that soweth to the Spirit shall of the Spirit reap life everlasting" (Gal. 6:8). It is biblically absurd to deny the teachings of Jesus. The belief that a lawbreaker is entitled to the same liberty as the law-abiding person defies common sense.

What then are we to understand by the word *hell?* What did Jesus mean when He used it? Let us begin by noting that the King James Version of the Bible uses the word *hell* to translate words which, in the original Hebrew and Greek, did not mean what is now popularly meant by *hell*. These words are the Hebrew *Sheol* and the Greek *Hades*. Sheol or Hades was the abode of *all* the dead. The part of Sheol where the wicked dwelt was called *Gehenna* or *Tophet*, meaning "place of burning," and the part where the righteous dwelt was called *Paradise*.

Psalm 16:10 is translated, "Thou wilt not leave My soul in hell; neither wilt Thou suffer Thine Holy One to see corruption." In his Pentecost sermon (Acts 2), Peter quoted this as a prophecy of Christ's resurrection from the grave. Many new translations simply leave the word *Sheol* or *Hades* in its original language. Others translate it "the grave."

Sheol or Hades is not always pictured as a place of dreadful torment but rather as the place where the dead live on, some like the rich Dives in torment and in punishment, and others like the beggar Lazarus in the bliss of "Abraham's bosom." Thus there was a separation between the righteous and the evil, with a great gulf fixed between (Luke 16:19-31).

God's Garbage Heap

What then does it mean for a soul to be cast into hell? The answers come from two directions, the teachings of Jesus and the ugly history of sin.

1. The teachings of Jesus. Eleven times in the Gospels our Lord mentioned hell as a place of future and eternal punishment. In every instance the word He used was *Gehenna*. There is a history to this fearful word. Just behind Jerusalem, under the southwest wall, is a steep ravine. It is called the *Valley of Hinnom*. The Jews had a shorter name for it. They called it *Gehinnom* or *Gehenna*.

In the early days of Israel, before our Lord's time, that valley was the scene of many shameful idolatries. Heathen gods were worshiped there. The altar of Moloch was there where children were sacrificed in fire (2 Chron. 28:3; 33:6). When the reformer Josiah came to the throne, these unspeakable cruelties were swept away. The altars were overthrown and the images ground to powder. From that time forward, the location was pronounced unclean forevermore and became the garbage dump of the city.

In Christ's day it was still the scrap heap or the nuisance ground for Jerusalem, where the refuse of the street, human excrement, and bodies of dead animals were dragged and left to rot. Sometimes as a special mark of shame, the Sanhedrin ordered the dead body of a criminal to be flung into Gehenna. Jackals prowled about the valley by night, and maggots fed on the refuse and rubbish. To prevent disease it was set afire, and the smoke of the valley ascended up by day and by night, for the fires were never quenched. The Jews looked on it as the final destination of everything repulsive and outcast. With a knowledge of this, our Lord described Gehenna (hell) as a place "where their worm dieth not, and the fire is not quenched" (Mark 9:44,46,48).

Gehenna became the place of deepest shame, and with the use of this terrible picture, Jesus chose to portray the final destiny of guilty and unrepentant people.

What this garbage heap was to Jerusalem, hell will be to the great universe of God. It is a ghastly picture. But though the pit of Gehenna is used as a figure of speech, let no one suppose that hell is not real. The Bible describes hell as a place of dreadful punishment reserved for the devil and his angels and for sinners who never repent (Matt. 25:41).

Behind the figure is a fact more terrible than human language can portray. Here is the picture of a great spiritual disaster, describing the final issue of sin. What does it teach us? The lesson is that spiritually a man may make himself a piece of refuse in God's great universe. A man may resist the divine plan and the divine love until he is cast out at last as waste, flung out in shame on the garbage heap.

Sin, in its final issue, brings a remorse that will gnaw the soul as worms gnaw corrupting flesh. The intensity of that final issue of sin, with its extreme suffering and punishment, cannot better be portrayed than by the flaming of fire.

But fire is not the only figure used to picture hell. The New Testament writers described the *lost* as "wandering stars, to whom is reserved the blackness of darkness forever" (Jude 13); and as being in "outer darkness!" (Matt.

8:12). What a dreadful thought! To be in outer darkness may mean not only that they shall be separated from God, suffering the loss of fellowship with Him and with His redeemed, but that they will be absolutely alone forever. In outer darkness they will not be able to see each other. To be forever in the loneliness of their own thoughts, with all their desires and no fulfillment, with memories of wasted opportunities and unfulfilled possibilities, with the anguish of regret—this is punishment beyond the searing of a flame of fire. Alone forever in outer darkness!

All men cannot have the same destiny in the world unseen. There is a separation between good and evil, between the Christlike and the Christless. There is a great gulf fixed. Who separates them? They separate themselves from God. The chasm is made in this life.

Men make different responses to the pleadings and warnings of the Saviour. Why is this true? It is not that God loves one above another. The truth is that God has no way of getting a man into heaven when he has hell in his heart. Hell is the burial place for those who are dead in trespasses and in sins.

2. *The history of sin.* From the ugly history of sin in our earthly experience, we can get some idea of what it means for a soul to be cast into hell. The reality and true nature of hell can be faintly glimpsed if we open our eyes to the effects of sin around us in this life. Sin has made a hell of this life for many.

We have all met people who were in the depths of agonizing remorse, scourged by the whips of conscience until physical pain would have seemed a luxury. There is really nothing so terrible as the pangs of an awakened conscience. But these are mere glimpses of what hell is like, and they demonstrate clearly that the outcome of sin is punishment and suffering. If the result of sin is so in this life, what authority have we to think it will not be so in eternity?

We who believe what the Scripture teaches about eternal punishment are frequently pitied by people who ask if we would take a child, or even an animal, and put it alive into a fire and watch it burn. Of course the answer is No. Then how can we believe in a God who is more brutal than we would be? How can we believe in a God who could be so vengeful as to decree eternal punishment? "This is the God of the Middle Ages," they say. This concept of God has been long abandoned. The modern idea of God is sugar and spice and all things nice! Such persons are trying to invent a God who measures up to human standards!

You Choose Heaven or Hell

The fact is, God does not put people into hell. They put themselves there. In his *Institutes,* John Calvin described the destiny of unbelievers in these words: "Now, as no description can equal the severity of the devine vengeance on the reprobate, their anguish and torment are figuratively represented to us under corporeal images; as darkness, weeping, and gnashing of teeth, inextinguishable fire, a worm incessantly gnawing the heart. For there can be no doubt that by such modes of expression the Holy Spirit intended to confound all our faculties with horror—and fix our attention on the calamity of being alienated from the presence of God."

Neither does God put anyone into heaven. By his choice he puts himself there. It is not God's will that anyone should perish but that all should come to Him in repentance (2 Peter 3:9). But all around us there are those who reject His provision of love and are, therefore, "dead in trespasses and sins" (Eph. 2:1).

Yes, we have a God of infinite love and goodness, full of grace and mercy. Where sin did abound, the grace of God did much more abound (Rom. 5:20). But God is also a God of holiness and righteousness and justice, and all His attributes are fulfilled in righteous dealings with His creatures.

Concerning the lost, Christ said, "These shall go away into everlasting punishment" (Matt. 25:46). They follow the law of their own lives. Of Judas it was said that he turned aside from his apostleship and ministry "that he might go to his own place" (Acts 1:25). This meant the place he had made for himself.

Some people think that if God wanted to do so, He could overlook wrong and benevolently take all the wicked into heaven. But if this were so, He would do violence to His own justice and holiness. The barrier to this is the wicked man himself. Since he chooses hell, it would be no kindness to put him in heaven. He would suffer in the presence of God. When such a one shrinks from God's presence here and shuns the presence of God's people by his own choice, how could his presence in heaven be agreeable to him or to the company of the redeemed? Yes, it is true that God has no way to get a man into heaven if he has hell in his heart.

If there is any difference between good and evil, if there is any difference between right and wrong, if there is any moral basis on which the world stands, we must believe in the issues of both. For those of us who know and trust in Christ Jesus, the reality of both heaven and hell is not open to debate. Our Lord made it certain.

Because of that certainty, Paul wrote to the church at Thessalonica, comforting them in their persecutions and assuring them that their day of victory is coming, a day that will be terrible for the unbelievers. "The Lord Jesus shall be revealed from heaven with His mighty angels, in flaming fire taking vengeance on them that know not God, and that obey not the Gospel of our Lord Jesus Christ; who shall be punished with everlasting destruction from the presence of the Lord, and from the glory of His power" (2 Thes. 1:7-9).

12

What Is Your Hope for Heaven?

After a brilliant sermon that greatly inspired the congregation, the pastor took his accustomed stand at the exit to greet the people as they left the church.

One by one they shook his hand with an appropriate expression of appreciation for the sermon of the morning.

In the crowd was a business executive who said, "I liked your sermon. It was well done and one of the best I have ever heard. I thank you for it. However, if you were in my employ, I would have to fire you."

The minister was surprised and somewhat crestfallen, but he waited for the explanation. It was not long in coming. "You have me sold completely, but you didn't close the deal. You walked away without the order."

It is one thing to marshal all the arguments about our hope for the hereafter. It is another thing to "cinch" the order and to ask, "What is *your* hope for heaven? And if you have such a hope, on what does it rest?"

The Christian Hope

The Christian doctrine of life after death and resurrection of the body rests first upon the truth of Christ's resurrection, and second, on divine revelation made by the risen Saviour and those who, by the Holy Spirit's leading, interpreted this message to us in the writings of the New Testament.

For a Christian, the final glory of heaven will be his only after the resurrection of the body and its reunion with the soul. But in the meantime, the soul has not entered the state of unconsciousness or sleep, nor has it passed out of existence; but it is absent from the body and present with the Lord (2 Cor. 5:8).

To the person whose final authority is the book of science, the world to come is an unfathomable mystery; but to us Christians it is not. The empty tomb, and the revelation given us by Christ Jesus and His holy apostles, has lifted the veil and assured us that "if our earthly house of this tabernacle were dissolved, we have a building of God, an house not made with hands, eternal in the heavens" (2 Cor. 5:1).

We Christians live by faith. Nothing that transpires in our lives today has its full explanation here and now. But a day is coming when we shall interpret all these things in perfect light, with all the clouds rolled away.

The events that took place on the day we know as Easter have literally changed the life and thinking of mankind and given us, for the first time, a real hope for the hereafter. By the word *hope* we mean more than wishful thinking. The dictionary defines *hope* in two ways: "To entertain an expectation of something desired; also to trust or rely on—to look forward to with confidence." "Happy is he . . . whose hope is in the Lord" (Ps. 146:5).

Our hope for heaven is not a vague fancy or an imaginary reverie. It is an expectation based on a revelation from God, demonstrated by an historical event, the resurrection of Jesus Christ from the dead.

On the night of His crucifixion, the disciples had disappeared from the scene. Peter had denied that he ever knew Jesus—this to clear himself of the charge that he was a "fellow traveler." The other disciples seemed to be in seclusion. To all intents and purposes, Christianity was as dead that night as the leaves on a painted canvas.

Some women of Galilee apparently had more courage than the disciples. They went and saw the tomb where the body of Jesus had been buried. But they went, without expectation or hope, to anoint a dead body. When they found the tomb open and empty, they did not stop to investigate but hastened to tell the disciples. Peter and John classified this information as "idle tales," satisfied that these women were understandably overwrought and perhaps unbalanced in their emotions.

However, the disciples went to see and came away convinced. From that moment a great change came over them. Their fears began to vanish and a new courage sprang up in their hearts.

Pentecost

Fifty days after the Passover, the Festival of Pentecost was observed. Great crowds were in the city, having come as pilgrims from all over the Roman world. This was a high holy day, a harvest-home celebration comparable to our Thanksgiving Day. On that day and to that crowd, Peter preached; and in his sermon he explained the resurrection of Jesus Christ. "Men of Israel, hear these words. Jesus of Nazareth, a Man approved of God among you by miracles and wonders and signs . . . you have taken, and by wicked hands have crucified and slain; whom God hath raised up, having loosed the pains of death because it was not possible that He should be holden of it" (Acts 2:22-24). That statement was made by Simon Peter, the same who at first thought the report an "idle tale."

During those fifty days there had been ample time to investigate the story. By "many infallible proofs" (Acts 1:3), the resurrection of our Lord had been attested. The New Testament writers describe eleven appearances of Jesus in bodily form after His crucifixion, death, and burial. On one occasion five hundred people witnessed His appearance at once, and they could not all have been hallucinating!

If the enemies of Christ had stolen the body, they could have silenced the voice of Christianity forever by simply producing it and refuting the disciples' claims. But they did not because they could not.

If the disciples had taken the body away and hidden it, it is difficult to believe that they would have died for a proposition which they knew to be a hoax. Men will be martyred for a conviction, but not for what they know to be deceit.

The resurrection of Christ became a dominant doctrine of the early church, observed on the first day of the week in evidence of its importance in Christian thinking. Here is news that has changed the world, producing the purest fellowship, the strongest brotherhood, the noblest characters, the finest architecture, the richest art, and the most inspiring music that mankind has ever known. Is it possible that all these blessings have grown out of a false report?

If the Resurrection is true, we have a guarantee of life

after death. If it is false, we do not have a shred of hope for the hereafter. "If Christ be not raised, your faith is vain; you are yet in your sins. Then they also which are fallen asleep in Christ are perished" (1 Cor. 15:17-18).

The Solid Ground of Hope

Some years ago in the days before World War II, a German theologian prophesied that the hope of heaven would count for less and less in religion and would ultimately disappear. The general trend of thought among those who minimize the scriptural revelation is that what happens beyond this life is trivial compared with the hope of achieving social reform and getting things put right here and now.

However, in the teachings of Jesus, the hope of heaven is not anything secondary, but basic and essential. We are all made with capacities for knowledge and truth and happiness and goodness and love. These capacities extend beyond the limit of our present state. They exceed our grasp in this brief life. We have but touched the hem of their garment.

To suppose that we are endowed with such capacities, though only partially developed in this life, and that suddenly they are all terminated in death, is to conclude that there is no rationality or purpose in life. To believe in God is to trust that there is an ultimate rightness in things—an ultimate distinction between right and wrong, and an ultimate vindication of the righteous and a nemesis for every crime. If any man can shuffle out of the consequences of his deeds by simply dying, then the power that conducts the world has lost control of things, and life has no meaning at all.

But for those who accept and receive the revelation of

God in Christ, there is solid ground. To know God in Christ Jesus is not only to have a rationale for life, but to know there is a purpose and a righteousness and a love that sets its desire upon all of us. We are brought into a relationship with God in such a way that He is afflicted in our afflictions, wronged in our wrongs, wounded and grieved by our sins. He was crucified on a cruel cross, and through the gates of death sought us to be His children, never to be separated from His love. Heaven is the final abode of those who have been justified and redeemed by God's saving grace.

If our trust is in God, and we are justified by faith in His Son, then we have peace with God through Jesus Christ our Lord. This relationship is the surest foundation for the life to come. That is our hope for heaven.

When we speak of our hope for heaven, we are not using the word as the world commonly uses it. In preparation for marriage, a young girl used to do a lot of sewing and collecting towels and sheets and garments that would insure a good start in housekeeping. This used to be known as a trousseau or a hope chest. But even with this there was often a lot of uncertainty. So much so that it was sometimes called a "hopeless chest." We do not use the word as a student who has taken a test and who sighs deeply saying, "I hope I passed." Our hope is really a confidence, a conviction, based not on a fervent wish, but on the faithfulness of God who cannot fail.

> My hope is built on nothing less
> Than Jesus' blood and righteousness;
> I dare not trust the sweetest frame,
> But wholly lean on Jesus' name!

On Christ the solid Rock I stand,
All other ground is sinking sand.

We do not stray into the blessedness of heaven. We prepare for it, and for it we are prepared. Heaven gets into us before we get into it. We are counting on a future life of joy and gladness, but have we ever tasted its joy and gladness here—the joy of the forgiven? We hope to meet our loved ones whom we have loved and lost a while, but do we trust the Christ they trusted and love the Lord they loved?

There are very few people who do not hope to enter the gates of that celestial city when this brief life is ended. The question is, are they on the right road? Have they, like Bunyan's Pilgrim, forsaken the city of destruction, passed through the wicket gate of repentance, and knelt at the cross where the burdens are rolled away? It is not in the power of man to say we can come in another way. There is no other way! Nor can we say we come tomorrow, for no man can be sure of tomorrow. "Now is the accepted time. Behold, now is the day of salvation" (2 Cor. 6:2).

The Security of Hope

What is your hope for heaven? Is it merely speculation? Is it wishful thinking? Paul wrote to the Roman church, "If thou shalt confess with thy mouth the Lord Jesus, and shalt believe in thine heart that God hath raised Him from the dead, thou shalt be saved" (Rom. 10:9). Without such a belief in His resurrection, there can be no personal salvation, and without salvation there can be no hope for the hereafter.

When the dark curtain falls, the lights go out, and the house is empty, in the night and silence of death, our only security rests upon what happened on that first day of the week at Joseph's garden tomb.

> He is risen.
> He is risen indeed!
> Alleluia!